F-28

The Edges
of Language

Also by Paul M. van Buren

Theological Explorations
The Secular Meaning of the Gospel

The Edges of Language

of Language

An Essay in the Logic of a Religion

Paul M. van Buren

SCM PRESS LTD

334 00369 5

First British edition published 1972
by SCM Press Ltd, 56 Bloomsbury Street, London

© Paul M. van Buren 1972

Printed in Great Britain by
Western Printing Services Limited, Bristol

Contents

To
Alice
Ariane
Philip
Thomas

Preface

This study has its roots in six years of rethinking the problem which I posed for myself in *The Secular Meaning of the Gospel*. The reviews, letters, and conversations of many have helped me on my way, but I owe special thanks to the John Simon Guggenheim Foundation for a fellowship, the Hays-Fulbright Commission for a senior lectureship, and Oxford University for an appointment as a visiting professorship during the year 1967–68. I had promised myself—and proposed in grant applications—to work out during that year the implications for Christian theology of Wittgenstein's *Philosophical Investigations*. The task has taken much longer, and it is only with this book that I attempt to make good on that promise. I should also like to take this opportunity to express my thanks to Haverford College, for it was in developing and defending two lectures given there in the fall of 1970, under the Mary Farnum Brown Library Lectureship, that I finally formulated the description which has provided the focus for and given direction to this study. Much of the writing was done on a study leave provided by Temple University.

If this book is readable, credit is largely due to an able editor, Dr. Anne H. van Buren. If the argument holds up, I owe thanks to the detailed criticisms of Dr. Thomas Litzenburg, who read an earlier draft of the manuscript and did his best to save me from making many a mistake. I dedicate this investigation to four more or less logical critics of religion who have taught me much about the edges of language.

Paul M. van Buren

November 1971

Introduction

Neither among believers nor among philosophers of religion has there appeared a consensus about the nature of religion. The discordance may be defined as a failure to reach agreement about what is going on when religious people speak as they do. Judging that an advance in understanding in this area depends upon finding a fresh way of looking at the matter, I am going to propose and develop in this book a new analysis of religious discourse.

I shall not presume to claim, of course, that this analysis will cover everything that we call religion. We use the word 'religion' for such a diverse family of cases that no single definition, much less one analysis, can hope to cover them all. I do not even claim that my analysis will fit all the various forms which history has produced of the religion with which I shall be concerned, Christianity. Religion, whatever else may be said of it, is a human affair, situated always in time and place. As a phenomenon of history, it has no more remained un-altered through changing times and circumstances than any other of men's affairs. In order to talk about actual religion, therefore, we must talk of someone's religion.

The religion that I shall analyze is that of educated Christians in the West in this last third of the twentieth century. By "educated," I mean that they have some knowledge of the history of their own culture, being aware not only of its earlier forms, but also of the great changes through which it has gone during the past few centuries. By "Christian" I mean that they consider themselves to be Christians, that they know something of that tradition, and that from its language, images, literature, and the cultic and other activities of the churches, they derive important insights into their own lives and the life of their society. As both educated and Christian they are, I shall assume, not unaware of the somewhat puzzling character of religious discourse, puzzles which have led many educated persons to abandon Christianity as irrational. Not all intelligent people, however, have felt themselves forced to make that move. When Bultmann, Bonhoeffer, the Verification Principle, and Vatican II are all acknowledged and given their due, the fact remains that Christians, both Protestant and Catholic, continue to exist. It is their contemporary pattern of Christianity that will be our concern.

In undertaking an analysis of religious discourse, I shall be maintaining that to describe this religion as a form of linguistic behavior is to focus on its central feature and therefore to present it fairly. There is no need to deny that religion is more a matter of how men live than how they talk. However, what I shall argue in defense of my approach is that a human form of life is precisely linguistic, that it is the fact that language is woven into all the rest of our activities that makes those activities distinctively human and, also, that gives our language its peculiar character. Our human language is not simply a collection of words, I shall argue, but our distinctively human way of going about the whole business of life. If discourse is to be our subject, then it must be the living talk of human beings using language together in the actual business of life. Otherwise we should indeed be far removed from the possibility of understanding this or any other religion.

To propose an analysis is to offer a description. Analyses of religious discourse presume to be descriptions, suitably objective and detached, of the workings of language as used by religious people. In this undertaking, however, the line between analysis and advocacy has been difficult to maintain.

All too often the analyst sets out to describe, simply describe, the actual workings of religious discourse, and ends by seeming to tell us that we were actually doing something different from what we thought in speaking as we did. This failure does not arise, I believe, from the personal nature of the issues involved. The apparent lapse from rigorous standards of analysis is, rather, the result of beginning with the mistaken idea that there can be such a thing as a pure description. Pure description is as hard to find as pure fact. Descriptions are people's descriptions in particular circumstances and developed for particular purposes. Once we drop the impossible requirement for purity of description, we can perhaps take the more modest line of seeking a description, the conditions of which are as open to view as we can make them.

Since I shall be proposing a new analysis I shall be offering a new description of the workings of religious discourse. A new description of anything, however, presents us with a new view of the matter, a new way to understand it. If I come to have a new understanding of Christianity, for example, then I may also be said to have come to have a new or different Christianity. This is true of any subject: to accept a new description of X is to see X in a new way, to have a new understanding of X. But if I understand X in a new way, then X is to that extent different for me from what it was before. To argue for a new analysis of religion, then, is unavoidably to argue for a new understanding of religion, and thus to describe a religion that would be new in some respects. To this extent, at least, my analysis will be far from "pure" description.

On the other hand, my case for this analysis depends in no way on accepting or rejecting what have traditionally been taken to be the "claims" of religion. The description I shall offer, if not pure, will at least be such that it can be understood and even accepted without taking a stand one way or the other on the religion in question. If that can in fact be accomplished, I shall have done all I could wish in the name of "objectivity."

I do not wish to hide the fact, however, that in my view one of the principal assets of my analysis is that it enables us to circumvent the issue of theism *vs.* atheism. By "circumvent" I do not mean to evade a genuine issue, but literally, to go around it, to pass it by, to show that it is of no particular concern to a Christian. I believe my analysis will show that this issue is a false one. It is false in that the issue of theism, as it has been handled in recent philosophical discussions of religion, misleads us when we try to understand the role of the word 'God' in contemporary Christianity. Indeed, these discussions of theism seem to rest on a misunderstanding of a good deal of the use of 'God' in much of the history of Christianity. More importantly, the issue of theism itself arises from and assumes a view of language and its workings, and so a theory of meaning, which I shall argue is inadequate and untenable. There are, therefore, linguistic or philosophical as well as theological or religious grounds for rejecting the issue of theism *vs.* atheism, and I intend to show that those who have taken up this debate, on both sides, are off the track.

The central thesis, and the heart of my analysis, will be that religious discourse, in its most crucial and characteristic utterances, those in which the word 'God' is likely to be employed, takes place along the edges of language, at the farthest reaches of our rules for, or agreements in, the use of words. This particular linguistic behavior, then, may be thought of as speaking at the frontiers of language, a way (certainly not the only way) of behaving when we have reached the point at which we want to say the very most that our language entitles us to say, where we want to say as much as could possibly be said. When the religious use of the word 'God' is understood as a case of walking language's borders, the nature of the puzzles engendered by this talk will become more comprehensible, and reasons for rejecting the theistic issue will become clear.

In order to show this, I must first show that both the problem before us and the way to its solution are linguistic, that our question, being about certain reaches of our language, must be approached by an adequate awareness of the linguistic character of our humanity. I shall then argue that if we understand our language aright, we shall have to take into account realms of our linguistic existence not sufficiently explored, namely, those lying along the edges of language. It is in this realm, I shall argue, that religious discourse is properly to be located, along with other behavioral neighbors and near relatives, which are sometimes confused and often compared with religion. Finally, some of the major implications of this linguistic placing of religious discourse will be worked out, showing the adequacy of this analysis as compared to several important, current alternatives.

That in bare outline is the task that lies ahead and the course that will be pursued. I shall first present the problem and lay the foundations of the method, then present and develop my central thesis, which I offer as the key to the problem, and the final chapters will work out the solution. Solution? Are there ever solutions in philosophy, especially in the study of something as historically fluid as religion? Let us say at least that I intend to present a reasoned argument. It is offered as a possible constribution to whatever progress there can be in the analytic philosophy of religion, and perhaps also in contemporary theology.

CHAPTER I
The Problem of Religion

Like so much else in our world today, religion has become problematic. Not just particular political systems, but the very organization of society is being called into question. Not simply the present patterns of management, labor, and the professions, but the concept of work itself is being asked to show its credentials. Not just our present institutions, but the very concepts of education, art, the family—all these and more have become problematic for an increasing number among us. Questions are raised not only about what these institutions, arrangements, or understandings have been in the past, but also about what they ought to be in the future, and even whether they ought to be at all. In such a time, it is not surprising that Christianity is being called into question also, and not only by outsiders. Indeed, Christians themselves have taken a leading role in subjecting their religion to critical scrutiny, asking themselves and each other what they are able to accept of their own religious heritage, and what they are to make of what they can accept.

This questioning of religion, even when dramatized as a contemporary crisis of faith, is certainly not the culturally central phenomenon that religious doubt was a century ago. As Alasdair MacIntyre has reminded us,[1] the debates about

1. A. MacIntyre and P. Ricoeur, *The Religious Significance of Atheism* (New York: Columbia University Press, 1969).

7

religion and theism which followed the appearance of Darwin's *Origin of Species* were culturally crucial. Men felt that when the foundations of religion were shaken, the whole fabric of human society was endangered. In our time, however, some theologians can talk extensively and even joyfully about what they call "the death of God," and although a few may be disturbed, many more are only amused. Such talk merely conforms to the temper of the times, and even with considerable journalistic coverage it appears to have been no more unsettling than for some painters to proclaim the death of art, and less disturbing than professors of English literature proclaiming the death of the written word. Behind the simplistic journalism of such obituaries, there may be important signs of the cultural times, but the questioning of religion takes its place in this as one sign among many.

Yet for many religion remains an important matter. From its beginnings and throughout its history, Christianity, in its varying traditions, has dealt with what have been usually taken to be the largest and most basic questions of human life. From it men have derived their scale of values and they have sought to fashion their way of life in the light of its teachings. It has told them of the final issues of life and of death, the purpose and destiny of individuals and mankind as a whole. Whether true or false, the claims of Christianity have been thought to provide answers to such questions. For self-critical Christians, who would admit that their religion can no longer sustain a claim to provide answers to all life's questions, it remains an important source of insight into life's problems and possibilities.

The questioning of religion, by no means entirely hostile, exists within the most loyal circles of believers, often accompanying movements of renewal and reform. Those working to change Christianity, to bring it "up to date," appear to find older formulations of the tradition inadequate to the expression of a contemporary faith. They find its rites in need of revision. Above all, they appear to find the ancient claims of its doctrines, no matter how ambiguous on careful examination, far too clear and bold for the situation in which they find themselves. In sum, the voice of Christianity from the past reaches the ears of many contemporary educated Christians with a voice speaking too clearly of matters essentially ambiguous, too surely of matters not open to such knowledge. For many Christians today, traditional Christianity, or what they take traditional Christianity to be, and as it is often presented by those who think themselves competent to speak for it, is not so much wrong as too explicit. There are those who judge it to be simply false, of course, but for many it is not so much false as too presumptuous.

This uneasiness about the traditions of Christianity is related to our cultural context and reflects the cultural transformation which has taken place over the past few centuries, and which sets us off from the ages in which Christianity arose and developed. It has been argued that this cultural shift constitutes the whole problem, that we live in a secular age and that the spirit of this age is such that we cannot make sense of the old religious traditions which grew up in a prescientific era. Although I find so sweeping a diagnosis too simple, I think it is true that important shifts in our thinking have been taking place, and that these changes at least set the stage for the way in which we ask our questions. A brief summary of the important features of this cultural change, then, seems in order. [2]

The present times may be distinguished from the past in which Christianity flourished not only by the increasingly rapid rate of cultural, technological, scientific, and social change, but also by the different attitude which men are learning to take toward this experience of transience. The pages of political, philosophical, and religious history make it evident

2. For a fuller development of these features, see L. Gilkey, *Naming the Whirlwind* (Indianapolis: Bobbs-Merrill, 1969), chap. 2. Cf. chap. 2 of my *Theological Explorations* (New York: The Macmillan Company, 1968; London: S.C.M. Press, 1968), and my essay in T. Dean and J. Raines, eds., *Marxism and Radical Religion* (Philadelphia: Temple University Press, 1970).

that throughout most of recorded time, men have feared change and longed for permanence. The highest values were accorded to those things which were thought not to change, and impermanence was considered a sign of imperfection. Now slowly and only partially, we seem to be shifting our attitude. Change is beginning to take on greater value for us. Increasingly we come to approve of that which is able to change and adapt, as over against that which is static or stable. This shift may lead to greater flexibility in our institutions and practices, as we become more alert to the possibilities of experimentation and able to adapt to new situations, but it can also produce a sense of floundering and uncertainty, resulting in some quarters in a reaction of rigid conservatism. If sometimes it opens the way toward innovation in all areas of life, it can also produce a tendency to unrelieved immediacy, in which only the present counts and all concern for the past is lost. For better and for worse, however, it is part of what makes up our present cultural context. That this shift puts special strains on our Western religious heritage is obvious, for we have inherited a tradition which defined deity as unchanging and unchangeable, the best things being those that are eternal, the temporal being degraded as ephemeral. No wonder that religion has been intimately and essentially linked with stability and with conservative attitudes.

Another important feature of the contemporary situation is our increasing pluralism. By this I mean that we are becoming increasingly aware of the fact that our experience of the world is of many different sorts. Of course we have ways of unifying our experience—personal, political, economical, cultural, aesthetic, physical, or religious ways—but these ways are all different and no one of them excludes the possibilities of the others. This has undoubtedly always been true, but what marks us off from our ancestors is that we are aware of the plurality of our experience and of the fact that anything may be seen in more ways than one. There does not seem to be a single Archimedean point from which all the rest of our experience can finally be understood. The idea of one final truth, one supreme perspective, loses force with us as we become aware of the variety of ways in which the world is a world for us. In the religious sphere, consequently, we are not only more aware of the variety of religions and the variety within any one religious heritage, but—what is more decisive—we speak of the religious sphere, as over against other spheres of human experience and understanding. What may be looked at from a religious point of view can also be seen from a psychological, sociological, political, and economic point of view. Increasingly, as we become aware of this, we feel morally bound to leave open these other angles of vision.

The other side of the pluralistic coin is a growing sense of the relativity of all things and all our ideas and understandings. As we come to see that any matter may be looked at from more than one angle, we also come to think what is seen from each of these angles can have its value, can be true in its own terms. That is to say, every truth is relative to some particular frame of reference. Terms such as "in itself" and "as such" lose all purchase in a world in which any description depends upon a specifiable frame of reference. "Man as such" or "power in itself" are not parts of our pluralistically experienced world, where we meet only particular men under particular circumstances, where we consider some particular case of power under a particular aspect, relative to some specifiable frame of reference, such as political power or physical power.

It should be noticed that this fundamental relativism does not lead necessarily to an ethical relativism in which, since all values are relative, no distinctions should be made. Surely the relativity of values does not place them all on the same level. From what non-relative vantage point could that judgment be made? Although that sort of relativism is always possible, so are a more positive tolerance and greater empathy in which we judge more soberly because we are aware that we make each of our judgments in relation to one of many possible frames of reference.

To the features of transience, pluralism, and relativity, I will add only one more, since I do not intend to provide a comprehensive description of our cultural context but simply to remind ourselves of the time and place from which we are asking about the understanding of religion. This last aspect of contemporary culture is our increased sense of our own human responsibility for our lives and the course of this world. Whether we find a way in which to live together in peace or whether we blow ourselves to atomic dust, whether we control population or slowly crowd ourselves to death, whether we halt our pollution of earth, sea, and atmosphere or continue to choke ourselves into extinction, the decision rests in our hands. No fate or deity, we seem to be realizing, will settle any of this for us. We are slowly becoming aware, as men of the past hardly were, that our future will be of our own making. For good or ill, the responsibility for what happens to us is ours.

These remarks serve to indicate the situation in which the present questioning of religion is taking place, and the context in which we wish to understand the logic of the religion of contemporary educated Christians. Much more could be said, of course, about this cultural shift which has led to what William James called a revolution in the seat of authority. The revolutions in historical method, in the natural sciences, in our whole view of what sorts of knowledge are possible, have led us to believe that, in the plurality of our experience, convictions ought to be held only with the degree of firmness which the evidence and warrants allow. If we contrast this judgment with the traditional demands of religious faith for total commitment on little or no evidence, we are faced with a revolution in the morality of knowledge, in what we think we *ought* to believe to be true, which surely contributes to our asking questions about religion in a way different from that of the past.[3]

These shifts in our attitudes and understanding can lead to a new view of religion itself and, more specifically, they have

3. The conflict between this morality of knowledge and that of the Christian tradition has been analyzed by Van A. Harvey. See his *The Historian and the Believer* (New York: The Macmillan Company, 1966; London: S.C.M. Press, 1967/71), and "Is There an Ethics of Belief?" *The Journal of Religion*, January, 1969.

made possible a new way of looking at our Western religious heritage. The past of Christianity may be seen as a historical phenomenon, a long history of changing ideas and practices, offering answers to questions posed variously in various circumstances. A contemporary understanding of history, science, and philosophy leads to the awareness that our ancestors' concept of "orthodoxy" tended to ignore changing circumstances, forgetting that the orthodoxy of one period often became the heresy of a later time. If a sixth-century definition of orthodox Christian faith, "that which has been believed everywhere, always, by all men" were to be taken literally by men with our canons of historical judgment, they would have to conclude that such a thing had never existed!

To become aware of these differences between ourselves and our ancestors is to find unavoidable the question whether yesterday's religion can serve for today. In what we may call a pre-scientific era, religion itself was pre-scientific, with conceptions of authority and evidence which an educated person today finds unacceptable. Precisely the claims of immutability which commended it to men of another era make it questionable today. The claim to be the single, final truth for all men is difficult to digest for men who are increasingly pluralistic and relativistic, and Christianity's former stress upon the dependence of man on all-competent deity, who holds final responsibility for human destiny and the future of the world, rings hollow in the ears of men who are becoming painfully aware of their own responsibility for human life and the course of this world. Could such a religion really be ours today? No wonder so many have simply dropped it!

Finally, the question can be raised whether religion is the sort of thing that *could* be true. Perhaps it is a matter of taste, a matter of personal preference, a "picture-preference," as it has been called. Matters that are true or false are those in which there is some agreed method by which their truth may be established. The natural sciences have given our culture a staggeringly powerful model of how what is true and what is false can really be decided, because we have agreed to accept its method of settling such questions. But who can say how we should settle which of men's religions, if any, is true? And if we cannot agree on that, then surely religions are not the sort of things which can be true. They may be matters of preference or cultural conditioning, but the doctrines of religions seem immune from falsification, as they are also immune from verification. In which case, truth is hardly at stake.

Moreover, sociological reflection draws our attention to the finding that religion is a negligible factor in Western men's political or economic decisions. Religion has become less socially important, moving increasingly to the private sphere of personal taste and style. Counted amid the pluralities of his life, a man's religion matters less than his income, his education, or his political opinions. It matters less to society, less to others, and perhaps finally less to him.

All this the educated Christian has heard and pondered, for to be educated in our time means, at least partly, to be exposed to these questions and to the fields of inquiry in which they are liable to be raised. Religion being more closely aligned to history than to logic, such cultural considerations are surely in order.

There is a deeper problem, however. Cultural, historical, scientific, philosophical, and sociological considerations may be grounds for raising searching questions about religion today, but I find it difficult to escape the impression that something is seriously mistaken in this many-pronged attack. There is the minor bother that few are well-enough equipped in any one of these disciplines, not to speak of the others, to feel sure about the answers which have been proposed to these critical questions. What is much more bothersome is the fact that when all these objections have been heard, the religious man is liable to complain that he is being misunderstood. We need to take note of the fact, which Wittgenstein and others have noticed, that the religious man does not believe in that which his skeptical critic denies.[4] What the critic attacks seems

4. Wittgenstein, *Lectures and Conversations on Aesthetics, Psychology and ReligiousBelief*, ed. Cyril Barrett (Oxford: Blackwell, 1966), p. 55.

always to be aside the point, so that the challenge to religion which we have been reviewing seems to the religious man to be missing its mark.

Further, the challenge to contemporary religion frequently claims to be modern, to be based on recently achieved developments in historical method, scientific understanding, or philosophical subtlety. The historicism and scientism of the nineteenth century, it is assumed, are well behind us, and contemporary philosophy, so we have heard, has made what has been called "the linguistic turn,"[5] finding a new method of analysis with which to unravel old conceptual tangles. The way in which most discussion of religion today deals with what it calls "historical facts," "empirical evidence," and "the meaning" of certain words, however, hardly encourages confidence that we have made such great strides forward.

The feeling that the contemporary challenge to religion misses the mark, combined with the impression that contemporary skepticism sounds a bit shop-worn, leads to a suspicion that may warrant examination. The suspicion is that the whole modern questioning of religion, both by skeptical outsiders and by uneasy educated Christians, has its grounds in an ancient habit of thought, one which is open to serious question and which may be the ultimate block to understanding the logic of the religion which is our concern. The habit of thought to which I refer is one that lies at the roots of some of the oldest philosophies: the idea that a word is the name for an object.

This habit of thought, in spite of the work of Wittgenstein and Austin, has not died out, although recent philosophical developments may have made us more sophisticated about the workings of language. It may be realized, for example, that to argue about whether there ever was an Italian Renaissance is not at all like arguing whether there ever was a Dodo. The

5. Richard Rorty used this expression for the title of his anthology of essays selected to illustrate the latest revolution in philosophy in the English-speaking world (cf. *The Linguistic Turn* [Chicago: University of Chicago Press, 1967]).

issue is liable to be one, not of fact, but of the usefulness of employing the term "Renaissance" for speaking of a complex movement covering an expanse of time. Yet the old habit remains and we assume that the word "Renaissance" does, after all, refer to something. We know, of course, that "and," "if," "but," and "because" are used, not to refer, but to connect our other words in sentences. But when we come upon a proper name, then surely here is a word whose role is to refer to the bearer of that name. Did not Wittgenstein himself point out that "the *meaning* of a name is sometimes explained by pointing to its *bearer*"?[6] Too easily we ignore the qualifying "sometimes." We do not stop to wonder why Wittgenstein added that. Instead, we push right ahead with the simple case of John, the meaning of which we explain by pointing to John.

On this hastily constructed base, we proceed to a case that is presumed to be of the same sort. John is a name, and surely so is 'God,' we may think. He is referred to, spoken of, distinguished from others, called upon. Surely 'God' is a name. Where or what, then, is its bearer? Only here, not in how we reached this point, do we think we have arrived at a difficulty. Is not this the center of our contemporary questions about religion? But has it not always been the center of men's questions and doubts about religion? Yet little or no attention is given to the habit of thought and the unexamined assumption which produced the problem.

Religion has led men to "speak *of* God" and to "speak *to* God," a God who, it is said, acts, loves, and judges, and who therefore seems to be a personal agent in the world. However, it is notoriously the case that neither this agent nor the effects of his agency can be distinguished. If God is an agent, then his agency seems to have no ascertainable effects upon the course of this world. The religious tradition appears to use this word

6. Wittgenstein, *Philosphical Investigations* (Oxford: Blackwell, 1953), §43. (References to this work hereafter will be given as *P.I.*, with the number of the section, or of the page when the sections are unnumbered.)

as the name of we-know-not-what, and its claims about the effects of this agency are ambiguous to the point of being nonsensical. The word 'God,' then, seems to be utterly incoherent, and claims about God's agency seem to amount to no more and no other than the denial of those same claims. No difference can be specified which would give content to the claim that there is a God that loves us. In such a case, the moral duty of an intelligent man is to have nothing to do with religion.

While this line of thought is by now familiar, the fact remains that there is scarcely more than a terminological difference between it and that which would account for the writing of Psalm 79. What passes as a very modern atheism, therefore, turns out to be as old as the religion which it attacks. The question therefore arises whether this challenge is any freer than the position it attacks from habits of thought called into question by contemporary philosophy. If the case is as simple as this argument makes out, it would seem absurd to find, as we do, that a number of well-educated and intelligent men, perfectly aware of this old argument, continue to use the word 'God' in a religious way.

There are other grounds as well for asking whether this line of criticism has understood at all correctly the actual religious use of the word 'God.' Why is there no consideration given, for example, to the fact that this word comes through the tradition primarily in the context of a story or a collection of stories, that it is set in the context of myth, legend, narrative, and song, and not in that of propositions? Further, why has no attention been given to the paradoxical fact that men who have spoken religiously "of God," have also said that they knew not of what they spoke, that their words were inadequate, that indeed they did not know how to use this word properly? Is there not a strange disparity between the uncertainty about and the ambiguity in the use of this word among religious persons, and the assurance and clarity of its use in the argument that is central to contemporary doubts about or denials of religion?

I do not deny that there have been and still are some proponents of religion who have used the word 'God' with the same clarity and assurance as have modern critics of religion. (They are surely to be distinguished from those who use the word haltingly, although there is nothing particularly modern about *that* distinction.) Nevertheless, the fact of that other, ambiguous use of the word by religious men opens the question whether modern critics of religion, and also those who answer them in their own clear terms, are correct in their understanding of what is going on when a religious person uses this term. Their analysis seems inadequate to the subject matter.

The heart of the difficulty resides in the fact that the word 'God' has been used as if it were the name of a something-or-other, and we are therefore led to assume that its meaning would indeed be explained by pointing to or otherwise defining its bearer. Seduced by old habits of thinking of words as labels for things, we take up the religious question on that assumption and end with the denials of religion which we have mentioned.

I have suggested that the contemporary Christian may be uneasy with his received religious tradition because he thinks the voices from the past claim to know too much about these matters. Yet while that may be an important part of the cause for his uneasiness, it is balanced in part by uneasiness about the arguments of the critics of religion, even when it is he himself who employs these arguments. He suspects that if the past seemed at times to know too much, so does the present, and that perhaps both are missing the point. I can show grounds for that suspicion if I can show that it is not so much secularism or secular thinking which poses the principal problem for religion, but rather, a misunderstanding, the roots of which are not modern at all. The misunderstanding, I shall argue, stems from the idea that words are labels, from the view as old as Plato that if we have a noun, we ought to be able to specify that which the noun refers to or stands for. When we add to this a somewhat positivistic penchant for making either/

or distinctions, forgetting intermediate cases, we are on a
well-worn road to misunderstanding what is happening when
a religious man uses the word 'God.'

I am not arguing that religion has remained a constant and
has come under attack only because of recent misunderstandings. On the contrary, I am prepared to grant that yesterday's
religion may very well not serve for today. But that has always
been true. Christianity has been changing since its beginning,
the religion of the past constantly being adapted to the conditions of each new present. Once we see this character of
Christianity, we are released from the misconceived task of
trying to identify its unchanging essence, so it may be well to
remind ourselves of a few of those changes that have taken
place over the centuries.

During its earliest years, Christianity was transformed
from a Jewish sect, centered in Jerusalem, involving faithful
observation of the Law and worship in the Temple, into a
Hellenistic religion, with circumcision and much else of the
Law set aside, centered in small communities scattered through
Asia Minor and Greece. At the same time, there began another
important transformation from an apocalyptic community
whose back was turned on this world, to what became in time
the principal cohesive social institution of the Roman empire.
The changing role of bishops, the increased emphasis on the
role of the bishop of Rome, the rise of monasticism—all these
and much more are signs of changes in the practices and
beliefs of Christians, compared to which more recent changes
are perhaps less impressive. Certainly the shifts in belief from
the early spirit-Christology to the later *logos*-Christologies,
with the development of the distinction between *physis*
("nature") and *hypostasis* ("person"?), were changes of major
proportions.[7]

Because of this history of transformation and ever new

7. The extent and importance of these christological shifts are des-
cribed in the first section of chap. 2 of my *The Secular Meaning of the
Gospel* (New York: The Macmillan Company, 1963; London:
S.C.M. Press, 1963; Penguin, 1968).

reinterpretation, it is unreasonable to ask for the logic simply of Christianity, without respect to time and place. Some of the roles which this religion used to fill have been taken over for us by other institutions and understandings. While it had no serious competitors, this religion and its Bible provided accounts of the origin of the earth and of human life, and a basic explanation for "the way things are," in areas that are now more convincingly described, for Christians as for others, by geology, biology, history, astronomy, anthropology, meteorology, and so forth. Christianity, in any contemporary form, could hardly play the explanatory role it once did. For many centuries its explanatory function has been diminishing, and this has only happened more rapidly in modern times because of the recent rapid proliferation and refinement of specialized fields of inquiry, which provide in smaller spheres their own explanation and descriptions.

It has been argued that, because certain important explanatory roles have been reassigned to specific intellectual disciplines, Christianity has no further role to play. The choice is between Christianity as it once was and nothing at all. Yet how can we conclude that when something as complex as Christianity loses one of its functions, it then can play no role at all?

It could be objected, however, that there must be some limit to the changes which could occur, beyond which we could no longer call the transformed creature by the same name. This seems to be more a logical than a historical point. Certainly, few if any Christians of today would feel themselves in familiar surroundings if they were suddenly translated into the Corinthian congregation to which the apostle Paul sent his letters. The same point can be tested in another context: "there must be some limit to the changes which could occur, beyond which we could no longer call the United States by the same name." But radical changes of geography (from thirteen to fifty states), political structure (the development of political parties, the power of the Supreme Court to declare acts of Congress unconstitutional, the income tax), and patterns of self-understanding (from pilot model of self-determination to world policeman!) have already occurred, and we manage to continue to use the same name without difficulty.

Let us consider the logical point, for it has received forceful expression by none other than Pope John XXIII. In his instructions to the delegates to Vatican Council II, he urged the *aggiornamento* of the church, but, he warned, this should be done without departing from "the substance of ancient doctrine." Eric Mascall, expanding on this theme, argued similarly that although it is the proper business of the theologian to reformulate doctrine, it is his duty not to change the substance of that doctrine.[8] The requirement depends upon the distinction between the form of a doctrine and its substance, the first thought of as variable, the second as permanent. It also depends upon the possibility of identifying the substance of ancient doctrine, quite apart from its form.

The difficulty with this way of putting the requirement is that ancient (or any other) doctrine exists only in words. If the words are changed, there is a change, however slight, in the doctrine. A doctrine is what some body, group, or person has taught. It consists simply in what someone has said. If I say something slightly different, I am teaching something slightly different. The distinction between substance and form may suggest another distinction between what is said and the meaning of what is said, between words lying on the surface and their meanings hiding mysteriously behind them. But if there is any validity to the thesis that the meaning of our words is to be found by looking at the tasks which they perform, then the distinction between meaning and word will prove complex enough without expecting it to clarify the rather different distinction between form and substance.[9] The only way I can be sure to be faithful to the "substance" of ancient doctrine is

8. E. Mascall, *The Secularisation of Christianity* (London: Darton, Longman & Todd, 1965), pp. 1–4.

9. The first to point this out, to my knowledge, was J. C. Thornton, "Religious Belief and 'Reductionism,'" *Sophia* (October, 1966), pp. 3–16. For a more recent analysis of the weakness of Mascall's position, see Vernon Pratt, *Religion and Secularisation* (London: Macmillan and Co, 1970), pp. 51ff.

to be faithful to ancient doctrine itself, which is to say, by saying exactly what the ancients said. But then what is the sense of asking theologians or anyone else to reformulate doctrine? The demand is self-contradictory.

Is there, then, no essence of Christianity? Well, we may read what Christians have said Christianity is, but this has changed over the centuries. There is no single thread running through all that they have said, which all forms of Christianity have in common.[10] Christians have emphasized now one central core, now another, or they have defined that core in more ways than one. The way out of this puzzle may be to learn to look at the word 'Christianity' in another way. Like the word 'religion,' it is one of those many words which can be defined only by describing a large number of cases in which it is used. Wittgenstein drew our attention to this sort of word by speaking of games, which seem to have no one feature in common, although this does not hinder our using the word freely and usually without misunderstanding. We can always give a definition which will cover, say, card games, but it works only if we ignore other sorts of games. So we can give a definition of religion which will indeed cover some of the uses of the word, but when we consider the variations which have existed and do exist under the names of Judaism, Christianity, Buddhism, and Islam, leaving aside all the other religions, what single common feature can we point to? The definition of religion can be made specific by limiting the field, or made more inclusive by sacrificing specificity.[11] If, then, we are willing to limit Christianity to what we conceive it to have been in one time and place, a definition is conceivable; but apart from such a move, it is not clear how we could agree to define the essence of Christianity.

10. The common fact of the occurrence of 'Christ,' as well as other words that could be mentioned, is hardly an informative enough feature to define an essence of Christianity.

11. But cf. N. Smart, *Philosophers and Religious Truth* (London: S.C.M. Press, 1964, 2nd ed., 1969; New York: The Macmillan Company, 1970), pp. 123f., for an attempt to define the 'family resemblances' of religions.

We have pointed out, however, that Christianity has been changing all through history, as we should expect a living religion to do. We need not, therefore, be discouraged by the logical and historical difficulties in defining its essence. Instead we may say that Christianity is a word which covers a variety of ways of life, combined with their varying patterns of talking and of understanding the human situation in its narrower and wider respects. Both the content and the scope of Christianity have varied considerably in the past, and that should alert us to look carefully at its contemporary form without assuming that it will resemble in all points its earlier forms. It might, for example, involve a less than all-inclusive view of the world and yet be for its adherents important to their living and understanding. The pattern of a contemporary Christianity is a possible subject of investigation, a religion whose logic (as William James would say, whose "particular go") could conceivably be made clear.

In order not to prejudice our analysis from the start, however, we should avoid defining the religion of contemporary educated Christians too precisely at the beginning. If what we are to investigate is one pattern of Christianity, I shall assume that this religion will lead its adherents to use the word 'God' as a serious word, and that they will use this word in close conjunction with the word 'Christ.' I shall also assume that both words will be used in some connection with their occurrence in the Bible, a complex of stories, legends, poetry, history, moral teaching, and much more. I shall further assume that contemporary Christians will do certain things together, including (though not necessarily primarily) certain cultic acts. Creeds, prayers, and other traditional formulations, however, may matter less to them than conversations, but I shall assume that they will also share important understandings or insights about life and the world. How all this is to be understood, however, has yet to be decided.

It has been thought in recent times that a fruitful way in which to understand religion is to clarify what is going on when religious people say the things they do. Yet, as we shall see, this agreement to see religion as a linguistic activity has not led to agreement on the proper analysis of the religious discourse of Christians, not to speak of that of any other believers. To say that religion is in an important way linguistic behavior may be true as far as it goes, but it does not go far enough. The failure to develop an adequate analysis of religious discourse, we shall argue, is due not to some inadequacy in taking religion as linguistic behavior,[12] but to a failure to think through thoroughly what is involved in approaching the subject in this way. Before developing the foundations for what may be a more adequate analysis, therefore, we shall review some of the major analyses which have been made so far and see in what ways they fail to do the job. The question that still needs an adequate answer, is, in its least prejudicial or question-begging form: What is going on when a man uses the word 'God' in a religious way? We turn next to some representative attempts to answer this question.

12. So Gilkey, for example, concluded. See *Naming the Whirlwind*, pp. 268, 272, 277.

CHAPTER II
The Problem of Religious Discourse

For over twenty-five years now, an increasingly active discussion has been going on in an attempt to understand religion by examining what believers say. A religious person will presumably say things which an unbeliever will not. He may say, for example, that we are not alone in the universe, that often in spite of appearances there is One who is with us and for us. He may say that we have our life as a gift from God and that we owe him love, obedience, and thanksgiving. He may say that the secrets of all hearts are known to God, who is alone the final judge in Jesus Christ. Such utterances are superficially like, "BOAC takes good care of you," "The Congo was the King's gift to the Belgian people, for which they were thankful," and "The Internal Revenue Service keeps track of all our income and is the judge of how much tax we must pay," and yet they are surely different. When the Christian says such things, what is he doing? Is he presenting us with a picture of the world, some of the essential features of which are different from those of the world seen by secular eyes? If so, is this picture true? How could we decide which picture is true? Are these even the right questions to ask? Such are some of the problems which have been discussed.

Of the various approaches to the problem of religious discourse, I shall discuss three which seem to be representative of much that has been written on the subject. Each sees religion in a different way, and each has difficulties of its own. First we shall look at the position that takes religion to be about the facts of the universe, of which the first is God. The second view takes religion to be a commitment to a way of life. The third regards religion as a quasi-metaphysical belief.

Those who have argued that Christians make factual claims have had in mind such utterances as "God exists," "God created and sustains this world," and "God loves us as a father loves his children." These utterances are taken to be descriptions of the state of affairs in the world. Talk about God is talk about a discrete individual of unique qualities, who acts as a free agent in or on the universe, and whose existence is the first or most important fact of this universe. This God has been defined by one interpreter of religion as "a Being which is unique, unitary, incorporeal, infinitely powerful, wise, and good, personal but without passions, and the maker and pre-server of the universe," whom it is none the less possible for men to disobey.[1] Antony Flew maintains that this "minimal definition" of God, which he says is that of "conservative theism," is the traditional Christian one. Christianity, in short, is taken to be, essentially, Christian theism. The same concep-tion of Christianity could also be expressed by saying that it is basically a belief in a particular (theistic) scheme, on which the whole religion depends. To be a Christian is to believe that there exists a God, who is the first fact of the universe and the basis of all that exists.

This Christian theism, however, runs into two related diffi-culties. One has to do with the factual claims of Christianity, and the other has to do with its supposed first fact, God. To put it simply, if religion is supposed to be supremely relevant to life, as religious people claim, what actual difference does God make in this world? Does God's love for men amount to anything in life? Second, to what is the Christian referring when he speaks of God? Does the individual exist to which Christians refer with this word 'God'? Logically, the second

1. Antony Flew, *God and Philosophy* (London: Hutchinson, 1966), pp. 28f.

problem seems the more basic and has come to be the crucial issue in this understanding of religion, but since the problem of the factual import of religious claims has received the wider attention, we shall begin there.

If we assume with this first line of interpretation that Christianity is essentially a belief about the facts, about what is the situation in this world, then the claim that God loves us may be presumed to be affirming that the state of affairs is thus and not otherwise. The assertion that God loves us is logically similar to the assertion that wild bears like human beings and will never attack, for both purport to inform us about one feature of our world. If this assertion about wild bears is true, it will have consequences for any who meet wild bears, or who like to camp in areas where bears are to be found. It is not difficult to specify what would have to happen upon meeting a wild bear that would count as evidence against the truth of the assertion. That is why we call it an assertion and say that it offers us information about our world: it could be true or it could be false, and we can specify how that could be determined. When we turn to the case of the Christian, however, we run into the puzzling fact that he claims that God loves us, yet continues to maintain this in the face of almost any conceivable eventuality. It is not that he does not consider unpleasant events, such as the death of children, or something so staggering as the mass murder of Jews during the last war, to be irrelevant, but faith seems to be able to absorb a great deal of negative evidence. Although some men have been confronted with so much evil or so much suffering—their own or that of others—that they have finally abandoned their religion, the fact remains that many Christians have understood God's activity in such a way that they have insisted that no matter what happened, God's love should not be questioned.

The difficulty with this position is that it consists in maintaining that no conceivable event can be incompatible with the claim that God loves us. This results in a contradiction: for we cannot, without contradiction, say that God makes a difference in this world, and also that whatever happens in this

world, God still loves us. The reason for this conclusion is that
to affirm one thing is to deny its opposite. To affirm that God's
love makes a difference in the world is to deny that no difference in the world results from God's love. This challenge
of falsification is designed to show that a nonfalsifiable claim
cannot also be a claim about the state of affairs in this world.
The claim that God loves us, no matter what happens, is
unable to stand up to the challenge and is therefore hollow.[2]

To accept this criticism, but also to answer it directly, is to
accept the model of language which it assumes. The model
derives from those areas of discourse in which to assert that X
is so is to deny that X is not so. The point is a logical one and
in logic it works. If we discuss the physical world, then with
the appropriate qualification to ensure the identity of X, it
also works: to affirm that water boils at 212 degrees Fahren-
heit under certain circumstances is to deny that water does not
boil at 212 degrees, if the circumstances are the same. In considering religion as a belief about facts, the same (by no means
esoteric) model of factual assertions prevails. God's love for us
is taken to be a fact in the way in which human love may be
taken as a fact. I may say that I love someone, but there are
certain actions or patterns of actions which would show that I
do not in fact love him, and that my assertion of love is false.
On this analogy it is argued that if God's love is real, then it
must be possible to imagine a course of events which would
falsify an assertion of God's love.

The theist might reply that our behavior is too ambiguous
to count as decisive evidence for or against human love. Likewise, he might argue, the worst of circumstances can neither
prove nor disprove the love of God. But this argument will
not stand, for the God of theism, unlike human beings, is
omnipotent and perfect and is able to love us effectively, no
matter what happens. The argument fails, therefore, but it
does clarify what sort of fact God is in this interpretation.

2. Antony Flew, "Theology and Falsification," in Flew and Mac-
   Intyre, eds., *New Essays in Philosophical Theology* (London: S.C.M.
   Press, 1955).

God's existing in or over the universe is on a par with the laws of Newtonian physics; the assertion of his omnipotence or omnibenevolence is taken to be an assertion of the steadiness and reliability of his love comparable to the reliability of the law of gravity. But if God's love is supposed to be real, in the sense that gravity is real, then we ought to be able to specify what could show that God does not love us or that there is no God to love us. If we cannot do so, then clearly the claim that God loves us says nothing whatsoever about the state of affairs in the universe. It is not about the facts; it only pretends to be.

An example of this way of taking religion may be seen in the parable which Ronald Hepburn developed in order to throw light on the question of whether such religious statements as that Jesus was raised from the dead are matters of fact and of truth.[3] The parable is set in a concert hall, in which two persons notice and come to discuss a rectangle on the wall up in a distant corner of the hall. One says it is a window, and the other argues it is a painting. Once the lights come on and it is clearly seen to be a painting, the first person cannot go on saying, "To the eye of faith, it may still be a window." So, it is concluded, the resurrection of Jesus is either a fact of history and the divine vindication of Jesus, or else it is an illusion of the pious imagination.

The difficulty with this parable is that it does not fit the subject, and this could be because religion is understood as being about the facts. As a matter of record, the light of searching and reasonably unbiased historical investigation has been turned on the documents relevant to the resurrection of Jesus for some time now, and it has settled very little. The rectangle on the wall still being argued about is not the resurrection, taken on the same level as a man rising from his bed in the morning. The only historical fact which the historian is able to connect with Easter day is the faith of the disciples. They said, "He appeared" and "He was seen," but whether what they

3. In Ronald Hepburn's essay in *Metaphysical Beliefs*, ed. A. Mac-Intyre and Ronald Gregor Smith (London: S.C.M. Press, 1957), pp. 135f.

"saw" was a renewed and triumphant Jesus or a figment of their imagination is inaccessible to the historian. It is even wrong to say that the disciples claimed to have witnessed a historical fact, for not only did first-century Jews surely not use the word "fact" as modern men do, but it is evident that they understood "seeing the risen Jesus" to be different from "seeing the risen sun." The first "seeing" was always accompanied by conversion, and what was seen was never immediately recognized. On these counts alone, the risen Jesus could not have been of the same order as the risen sun.

The force of arguments that religious claims are factual in form but hollow in content depends upon an unargued assumption about language. The assumption is that making statements and describing have the places of honor in our linguistic activity. Stating and describing are assumed to have a unique relationship with facts and are the only linguistic activities which have untarnished claims to being labeled true or false. These assumptions, however, ignore the fact, which Austin pointed out, that calling an utterance true or false is actually an assessment of how well it does its job, and there are many more jobs done with language than stating and describing.[4] The assumptions about language on which this first interpretation of religion is based are therefore at least debatable and may well be wrong. If they are wrong, the interpretation itself may be wrong.

Attempts to meet the challenge of falsification on its own grounds, therefore, suffer from the same dependence on a suspiciously narrow view of language. This can be seen by looking at the well-known argument for eschatological verification.[5] What is worrisome about this argument, as we shall see, is not its weaknesses, but what we should have to accept if it worked, the picture of religion that would result from committing ourselves to the view of language as reaching its finest hour in the activity of stating and describing.

4. J. L. Austin, *How to Do Things with Words*, ed. J. O. Urmson (New York: Oxford University Press, 1965), p. 148. Cf. *P.I.*, §§241, 136.
5. The argument has been developed principally by John Hick.

The argument for eschatological verification accepts the theistic interpretation of Christianity which is fundamental to the challenge of falsification. It grants that Christianity makes claims about the facts of this universe and must be able, therefore, to specify how its claims could be tested empirically. But there is no difficulty here, so the argument goes, because when that theistic God puts an end to history and closes off this age, he will stand in the Last Great Day, empirically evident to the eyes of all. Anyone who can recognize a fact will be able either to see that Christianity is a lie, or to recognize God and see the truth of Christianity's claims. If this argument were to stand, then although we could not tell until the *eschaton* (the End) arrived whether Christianity were true or false, the religion that might or might not turn out to be true would be Fundamentalism, that highly rationalistic interpretation of religion that has come into fashion in some circles of Christians in several periods of history.[6]

The argument, however, has the weakness of trading illegally on a double use of its key term. There cannot be such a thing as eschatological verification in the sense in which verification has been demanded—or we could have it only at the price of denying everything Christianity has said about the *eschaton*. Verification and falsification are agreed procedures for settling matters within an agreed-upon frame of reference. Further, the language in which verification must take place if it is to take place at all is human language, under human conditions. That is the context implicit in the request for verification. What is to count as verification under the supposed but unimaginable conditions of the *eschaton* must be an unknown unless we forget what religion has had to say and invent a heaven that is a copy of our present circumstances. If Christian imagery of the *eschaton* makes any sense at all, however, it does so by insisting that we are not able to stipulate how matters will stand in that new state of affairs called variously heaven,

6. The point was made by Malcolm Diamond in his essay "Contemporary Analysis: The Metaphysical Target and the Theological Victim," *The Journal of Religion*, July, 1967.

the Kingdom of God, and the End.[7] The argument for eschatological verification is therefore invalid and, more seriously, constitutes a surrender to one particular way (admittedly a privileged way in our present secular culture!) of saying what is so and what is true or false.

Lately, discussion of religion as making factual claims has shifted to the concept 'God,' and the challenge is being made that the concept is incoherent.[8] To make sense in talking about God, presupposes, it is argued, that the speaker and the hearer know what they are talking about, that they have some familiarity with the individual to whom the word 'God' refers. However, the difficulty is that the word either has no reference, or its referent cannot be identified. Since God cannot be pointed to, he would have to be identified with further concepts, by means of our language. But if we say that 'God' refers to "the creator of the universe" we only move in a circle: if we don't understand the first, how can we understand the second?

The same difficulty can be shown in the concept of revelation, the idea of God's making himself known by speaking to Moses or the prophets, for example. If God were to speak, how could we know it? Briefly (for at a later point we shall have to consider these in detail), the alternatives seem to be three: (1) We may assume that God speaks; but since he is utterly other than men, we cannot understand him, for we understand only human language. Consequently, there could be no self-revelation of the God of Christian theism. (2) God speaks, and by a miracle he might cause us to understand his divine language. But this is only a longer way to the same negative conclusion, for if we understand by a miracle, this understanding is radically unlike what we call "understand-

7. For an example of this insistence, see Karl Barth, *God Here and Now* (New York: Harper & Row, 1964; London: Routledge and Kegan Paul, 1964), p. 37.
8. E.g. Kai Nielsen, "In Defense of Atheism," *Perspectives in Education, Religion and the Arts*, Vol. 3, *Contemporary Philosophic Thought: The International Philosophy Year Conferences of Brockport* (Albany: State University of New York Press, 1970), pp. 127–56.

ing," and therefore it could not be distinguished from "not understanding." There might be revelation of a sort, then, but we should never know whether we understood it. (3) If God does speak and we understand, then he would have to speak human language. As we shall see later, however, understanding each other is not just a matter of words. Understanding presupposes using language as we do, which involves behaving as we humans behave. The God who could speak and be understood by men would have to be more than figuratively anthropomorphic. He would have to be an exceedingly human God. But that sort of God has been ruled out by the concept of theism that is under discussion and which is presumed in this first interpretation to be the central tenet of Christianity. If Christianity is indeed centrally committed to that sort of theism, then it centers in a conceptual incoherence which an intelligent person would not care to entertain.

Religion conceived as a theism expressed by statements of supposed fact would seem an unlikely possibility for educated Christians today. It is open to serious accusations of conceptual confusion, and if these objections could be met the result would be a religious fundamentalism that seems scarcely worth the battle. Better to "close up shop," as Kai Nielsen urges,[9] and grant that religion along with belief in witches and goblins has had its day and is hardly adequate to contemporary understanding.

Yet this whole discussion gives the impression of having left much out of consideration that is important to religion. It ignores so much of what has happened in Christianity, beginning with Schleiermacher's *Speeches on Religion*, that contemporary religion seems hardly to be the subject of discussion. Some twenty-five years ago, the present interest in the analysis of religious discourse was launched by John Wisdom's essay "Gods," with the opening sentence: "The existence of God is not an experimental issue in the way it was."[10] The

9. *Ibid.*
10. Reprinted in J. Wisdom, *Philosophy and Psychoanalysis* (Oxford: Blackwell, 1953).

far-reaching implications of that thesis have hardly been considered in the fact-centered, theistic understanding of religion.
The result has been that many feel that this approach has
missed the heart of the matter, even when they have not
always been able to give clear reasons for this conviction.
Some, however, have produced arguments to show that a
theistic interpretation of religion has mistaken the covering for
the real article. Their thesis has been that although Christianity may appear in theistic garments, it is in fact another animal
altogether. To this second line of interpretation we now
turn.

I have said that some have not been clear about why they
feel that religion is not factually theistic, but not Professor
R. B. Braithwaite. His essay, "An Empiricist's View of the
Nature of Religious Belief," is characteristic of the view that
religion is a commitment to a way of life.[11] No less than Flew
and Nielsen, Braithwaite is committed to the clarity which
characterizes the truth-testing procedures of statements of
empirical fact, scientific hypotheses, and the propositions of
logic and mathematics. He sees, however, that no sense can be
made out of religious discourse if we interpret it along any of
these three lines, for the assertions of the believer do not
depend, either directly or indirectly, upon empirical evidence,
since no specifiable state of affairs is considered by the believer
to constitute grounds for abandoning his faith. Nevertheless,
religious people think that their religion has a great deal to do
with the world; they do not believe in a self-contained system,
whose propositions, like those of logic, are true by definition.

There is, however, at least one class of statements which
falls outside the range of those three classes mentioned, the
argument continues, yet which is clearly important in human
life: the statements of morals, the principles of which serve to
guide human conduct. When a man says that it is wrong to
kill, he is not describing some fact written into "the order of

11. Cambridge, England: University Press, 1955. Reprinted in *The
    Existence of God*, ed. John Hick (New York: The Macmillan Com-
    pany, 1964) and elsewhere.

things," nor is he describing his own inner attitudes or emotions. He is describing neither an external, "objective" fact, nor an internal, psychological, "subjective" fact. He is, rather, *prescribing* what he intends to do and what he thinks others should intend. Prescription is not description. It is simply another linguistic act in which we engage.

Following this lead, this second way of understanding religion interprets what may reasonably be regarded as the central affirmation of Christianity, that God is love, as the assertion of an intention to behave in a loving way. That is said to be the actual use of this religious affirmation. Religion, however, has an additional feature which distinguishes it from morality: the believer associates his intention with a particular religious story, and it is the different stories, associated with the intention to behave in a certain way, that further distinguish one religion from another, even when the intentions correspond closely. The story, itself a collection of empirical assertions, need not be believed to be empirically true, for its function is to provide psychological support to the believer's intention. In sum, a religious belief is neither more nor less than an intention to behave in a certain way, together with the rehearsal or remembrance of particular religious stories.

Before considering the difficulties in this interpretation and the objections which have been raised, we should say that it does indeed account for the moral aspect of Christianity and does justice to the fact that religious conversion has always been thought of as a conversion of the will and as the beginning of a new way of life. Furthermore, since Christians have always held that their faith had ethical implications, the logic of this conviction is made clear by interpreting belief as itself a moral intention. On this account, it becomes clear why, for example, the conflict between the so-called Confessing Church in Germany and Hitler's program of totalitarianism and anti-Semitism, seemed to the confessing Christians to be absolutely basic, a conflict that touched the essence of Christianity. If Christianity is essentially a way of life, then the fundamental

conflicts will be moral ones, while the conflict between science
and religion, for example, will be judged to rest on a misunderstanding of either science or religion (or both) by one (or both)
parties. According to this second or moral interpretation of
religion, that conflict should never have arisen, a judgment
which a great many other contemporary believers share.

A number of objections can be and have been made to this
view of religion, however. In the first place, the role of "the
story" in Christianity seems inadequately described. To consider the story, whether the biblical story or the creedal story,
as only a psychological support to living the Christian life is to
do less than justice to what Christians have said and thought
about the story. We could strengthen this second interpretation by putting the story in a logically stronger position, as the
vehicle of the images and metaphors from which Christians
derive the principles by which they live. If at the same time we
broaden the conception of morals to include the larger and
looser, but no less important, judgments by which we determine what constitutes the good man, the good life, and the
good society, we might then propose that the story (for
Christianity we mean especially the story of Jesus, in the
context of the larger and more complex biblical story on the
one hand, and the further developments of the doctrinal story
on the other) is the source of, and inspiration for, the controlling images and values by which Christians live.[12] The controlling image of the Kingdom of God as the fulfillment of the
love of God for men, expressed in the story of incarnation,
suffering, death, and resurrection, could be regarded as the
complex by which the Christian assesses and relates to both
himself and the world.

So understood, Christianity would not offer an explanatory
scheme to be tested by evidence or compared to other
schemes. Rather, it would offer a story which may be read as

12. Such a correction is suggested in important contributions by
Ronald Hepburn and Iris Murdoch to *Christian Ethics and Contemporary Philosophy*, ed. I. T. Ramsey (London: S.C.M. Press,
1966).

an invitation to a way of life. The only way to "test" the story is to live it. It could be "true" only in the sense in which it may be "true" that it is better to give than to receive, more adequate, so some would judge, to our "humanity," clearly itself a term of value. This view of religion sees the word 'God' imbedded in a story, the function of which is not to describe the world. When the Christian speaks of the God of love and justice, the Father of Jesus Christ, he is not, according to this interpretation, telling us about some supposed transcendent being. His words refer us, rather, to a story whose controlling images provide the leads by which the Christian shapes his life. The story itself is not true or false in the way in which a historical account is true or false, but in the way in which one view of life is true or false. Furthermore, the story does not control the Christian's course of action as a moral principle controls the action of one committed to it, for the story is ambiguous (owing to its dramatic form), inviting the question whether the hearer or reader has ears to hear and eyes to see. This is why religious people may be committed to the central images of one story (and so we may say that they hold to the same religion), and yet be of two minds as to how to act in a particular situation.[13]

This interpretation of religion, even when amended to do justice to the role of religious stories and broadened in its conconception of ethics, is none the less open to a major objection. It is all very well to say that religion is not about matters of science but about how to live in the world, yet is that all it is? It seems arbitrary to say that when a man speaks of God, the word 'God' is only doing duty for a story from which he derives an intention. Surely this is to reduce religious claims to the status of moral affirmation, so that no claim is made at all. If the Christian says that God loves mankind, and someone

13. These points have been worked out in detail by Louis Hammann, "The Structure and Function of Religious Stories," unpublished dissertation, Temple University, Philadelphia, Pa. Cf. my *Theological Explorations* (New York: The Macmillan Company, 1968; London: S.C.M. Press, 1968), pp. 69–77.

else says there is no loving God, according to this interpretation they do not disagree about the world at all, but only in
their intentions and moral policies.

This charge of reductionism, however, should be used with
care.[14] In one sense, every theology is a reduction, since it is
an attempt to say what Christianity is about in some other
words than those which have been used before. As we have
argued, if reformulation is to take place, then it must consist in
changing the words, at least to some extent, and this amounts
to reducing the older words to the newer terms. If theological
work is to be done at all, the issue does not turn on whether
there is a reduction, but on whether a given reduction is
adequate.

What, then, is inadequate in the reduction of religious
assertions to the terms of moral commitments? The answer is
that such an interpretation denies that the religious man even
wants to say anything about the world in which we find ourselves, and this is so contrary to the evidence as to be absurd.
It is not enough, however, to realize that this mistake has been
made. More important are the reasons for it. Proponents of
the moral interpretation of religion were led into this error
because they were convinced by the arguments of those who
define religion as fact-centered theism and find it untenable.
But that means that both lines of interpretation depend upon
the same understanding of language. Both find that since
religious utterances are neither verifiable nor falsifiable, they
cannot be about the world. They differ only in that the inter-
preters of religion as moral commitment have found in pre-
scriptive discourse another model for understanding what
believers say, and one which does not pretend to say anything
about the world.

It has been objected, however, that this is not how believers
understand their own words. When Christians say that God is
love, that he has made himself known in Jesus Christ, that God
has made us for each other, that the wages of sin is death, that

14. Cf. J. C. Thornton's argument, "Religious Belief and 'Reductionism,'" *Sophia* (October, 1966), pp. 3–16.

he has forgiven us our sins in Jesus Christ, they have surely
understood themselves as at least *trying* to say something
about the situation in which we find ourselves. If these
utterances prove meaningless as empirical statements of fact,
can they have some other relationship to the facts? Unable or
unwilling to explore such a possibility, those who argue for a
moral interpretation insist that, regardless of what religious
utterances may seem to do, they actually function as declara-
tions or commendations of a commitment to a particular way
of life. That they *also* do this is not contested, but that they do
nothing but this seems difficult to accept and has led to a third
interpretation of religion, to which we now turn.

In objecting to the moral interpretation of religious utterances, John Wisdom insisted that "some belief as to what the
world is like is of the essence of religion."[15] On the face of it,
this seems to be right. Surely religious people are trying to say
something about what is so and what is true. But we can say
this, it seems to me, only if we are able to break out of the
narrow linguistic confines of the first two interpretations. It
is no good taking sides on whether Christianity involves
beliefs about how the world is, unless we first recognize that
"saying how things are" is not a simple matter. The difficulty is
not that we do not know how to say what the world is like,
but that we know how to do this in so many different ways.

One way of saying so is the factual one fundamental to the
first two interpretations of religion, like talking of tables,
chairs, trees, stones, and all sorts of other objects. This is of
great importance to us, obviously, because having bodies ourselves, we have to get along as happily as we can with bodies
other than our own. Since we find it less than satisfactory to
bump into tables, chairs, trees, and the rest, we find it useful
to inform, warn, and otherwise indicate to each other that such
an object lies just around the corner. More basically, as
Strawson has pointed out,[16] it seems to be of utmost utility to

15. J. Wisdom, *Paradox and Discovery* (Oxford: Blackwell, 1965), p.
54.
16. P. Strawson, *Individuals* (London: Methuen & Co., 1959).

us to be able to identify and reidentify the objects we come across, such as things we find edible and things that are dangers to be avoided. For these purposes, descriptions of objects play an important role in our lives, and we have various ways of finding out whether what we say about them fits the situation. Either a plant so described is or is not edible; either an animal is dangerous or not; either we can find an object where it was said to be or we cannot. Statements about and descriptions of objects, then, can be true or false, and this is one of the ways in which we talk about the world. It is not, however, the only way.

We also talk about persons, and Strawson has shown that talk about persons cannot be reduced without remainder to talk about objects. Talk about persons is always talk about persons who have bodies, of course, so that like objects, persons can be pointed out, described, identified, and reidentified. Yet our language about ourselves has the special feature of applying both to ourselves and to others, so that I can say, "I am tired," as well as, "He is tired." When we learn this way of speaking, we learn to look for external criteria in others as a sign that what we say is true; but we learn also that we do not need to look for external criteria when talking of ourselves. This interesting though utterly familiar feature of our talk about persons makes it different from our talk about objects.

To talk about the world, to say what is the case, is a human activity, the act of a person. Further, "the world" about us is the world about *us*, and the case is *our* case. It is an important part of our talk that we are interested in our surroundings not simply as in objects which are "there," but as in objects with which we have to cope. Furthermore, *our* context is also the context of our *person* and of other persons, which is logically different from the context of objects. Speaking of persons, of friendship or enmity, of trustworthiness or unreliability, is another but just as fundamental way of talking about what is the case, as is talking of weight and dimension. The question of whether a certain person is to be trusted is as much a question of fact (of course in a different use of the word 'fact'—

which is just the point!) as that of the strength of steel girders. If I say that John is trustworthy, I tell you that certain expectations about his future, or certain judgments about his past, are reliable. Our talk about the world is therefore richer than is dreamed of in the philosophy which defines religion as (incoherent) fact-centered theism or moral commitment.

Let us turn to a third way of talking about the world. It has been said that the world is a vale of tears, that the world is a stage, that the world is God's creation. These words too seem clearly enough to be about the situation in which we find ourselves, the context for all our dealing with matters-of-fact and with persons, and for all the other ways in which we come to terms with life. Life may be a tale told by an idiot, but it may also be a tale told in other stories, such as those of religion. If statement and description are ways of talking which bring us into matter-of-fact relationships with the world, then we could say that stories, by predicting and proposing, bring us into contextual relationship with the world. Perhaps this is the way to understand religion: religion proposes a way of looking at everything we have been looking at already. It proposes a way of putting it all together, and it depicts the world seen in this way. Christianity in its sacred stories gives nature a shape, or insists that nature does have a shape: it is cosmos, not chaos. History is arranged as a drama, with a beginning, a middle, and an end toward which it moves.

On this quasi-metaphysical reading of religion, Christianity gives an answer to the question: What is the world like? Although Christianity has nothing special to contribute to the physical sciences, it does have something to say about the world in its fully human dimension, as our total context. The question to which it gives an answer, therefore, is better put: How is it with us in this world? The way in which Christianity gives its primary answer to that question is by telling the biblical story. If the ambiguous character of stories results in this answer being ambiguous, the religious man can only insist that that is the kind of answer that is appropriate to that question.

This third way of interpreting religion sees religious belief as
a way of seeing what everyone else sees also. Religion so understood can be in no conflict with the findings of the natural
sciences, when the natural sciences seek only to describe
objects. Yet religion is about the facts, so that it can indeed
be in conflict with *some* other ways of looking at and speaking
of this world. Although it takes no sides on disputes about
whether the universe began with a "Big Bang," it takes sides
at once in a dispute about whether life is a tale told by an idiot
and therefore has no purpose or sense. Because this view of
religion presents it as a selectively interpretive scheme, we call
it a quasi-metaphysical interpretation of religion.

This third interpretation of religion has its limitation, however. We can argue that religious belief is belief about the
facts in this metaphysical or interpretive sense only if we waive
all claims to its being about the facts in a non-metaphysical
way. If religion proposes a way of seeing, it cannot also be
telling us that there is yet another thing to see, another object,
for example. Such classic utterances of religion as "the wages
of sin is death" and also "in my Father's house are many
mansions" and even "there is a God who loves us" may be proposing a way in which to look at our whole world, but they
are not telling us about hitherto unnoticed items in that world.
Speaking of God, then, turns out to be a special way of speaking of the universe that is around us. The conclusion would
seem to follow, however, that although this interpretation of
Christianity can make sense of religion as a sort of pantheism,
it provides no support for the theism for which it claims to
make room. God may be a controlling image, a fictional figure
in a certain way of talking about the world, but he can hardly
be the discrete individual which was so central to our discussion of the first interpretation.

It is worth noting that John Wisdom, whose essays suggest
the possibility of some such metaphysical view of religion, has
himself insisted that metaphysics can no longer be regarded as
a super-science which provides information about the basic
constituents of the universe. If talk of God is metaphysical,

then of course it will be immune to empirical falsification, since it is not talk about a fact in the way in which the first interpretation saw it. But it scarcely gets us beyond the second interpretation. There, we saw, talk about God was taken to be talk, not about God, but about the way of life to which the speaker is committed. Here it is about a way of seeing things to which the believer is committed. No doubt any Christian would want to grant that in some important sense he is committed both to a way of life and to a way of seeing the world in which he leads that life. But is either sufficient, or are the two together sufficient?

If we can stand back from the line of thinking of each and all of these interpretations and recall actual cases of serious religious belief, it will be evident that there is at least one feature of religious discourse that has been neglected in each interpretation. Religion, at its most serious level, I suggest, has almost always been marked by what we may call a sense of the mysterious. What I mean is that religious people have spoken guardedly when they spoke of God. They have said that God is ineffable; that he is beyond their understanding; that whatever they said of God was not, strictly speaking, true; or that their words were inadequate to their subject. How such language is to be accounted for remains to be seen, but it seems evident on the face of it that this is not typically how we speak of facts, of morality, or of metaphysics. We associate this way of speaking with the sense of mystery, wonder, and awe, and such speaking has been a not unimportant mark of religious men, at least in the Christian tradition.[17] Is all this to be ignored?

The first interpretation of religious utterances as statements of fact would consider the expression of wonder to be a clear sign of conceptual incoherence. The man who says he knows

17. Rudolf Otto drew attention to this feature in his *Idea of the Holy* in 1917. In agreeing that this is an important feature of religion, however, I am by no means committing myself to Otto's analysis of it or the consequences which he drew from it. These I shall work out in a rather different way in the later chapters of this study.

not of what he speaks is simply confused. The man who says his words are inadequate had best stop trying to say what he admits he cannot say. On the second interpretation, the halting character of such language is ignored, since religious utterances are considered to be perfectly clear when interpreted as expressing moral commitments. Nor is this stumbling character accounted for by the third interpretation. The paradoxes of some metaphysicians are not the same as the acknowledged obscurities of the religious. A characteristic feature of religious utterances is thus ruled out, or more or less frankly ignored, and at least to that extent, all three interpretations of religion would seem to be inadequate.

The failure, if such it be, of these various interpretations might be ascribed to the fact that they began by investigating religious discourse. This judgment, however, that language cannot provide an adequate entry to the subject of religion, assumes that these various interpretations are operating with a fully adequate understanding of language. If that assumption is correct, then their failure to provide a convincing analysis would be grounds for concluding that language is not the key to our problem, that it is itself no door to the understanding of religion in our time. I wish to challenge this assumption, however, by developing certain implications of the so-called "linguistic turn" which will provide tools more adequate to understanding religion. I shall therefore postpone further consideration of religion and turn to the fundamental task of getting clearer about the workings of our language.

CHAPTER III
A Review of the Fundamentals:
Our Language

Religion may be a problem for us in more ways than one, but insofar as it challenges our understanding, the problem arises in language. That is to say, our difficulty when we do not understand something presents itself as a difficulty in knowing what to say about it. Since we want to understand religion, and what the religious man says, the problem presents itself in words, and any solution to it will come in the form of words. The use of words lies, therefore, at the heart of our problem.

An investigation of words and our language, however, places us in a circular situation: the very language in which our problem is presented is also the only tool we have for solving it. This means that we are in a position like that of a man who wishes to examine the lenses of his eyes, yet must have those lenses in place in order to carry out his examination. Nor is there any way out of this circle: words are so centrally and inextricably a part of our life that there is no Archimedean point from which the puzzle can be unraveled. Only as linguistic beings can we set out to understand what our language is for us. Otherwise, we have literally nothing to say.

Our task, therefore, takes the form of becoming more sharply aware of what we know already. Since we all know how to use language already, we can expect no esoteric discoveries, yet because we are so familiar with the use of words that we take them for granted, we can learn something by making language itself a subject of attention. What we must do is look more carefully at the familiar, for it is our familiar language itself that entraps us from time to time and leads us into puzzles such as those we considered in Chapter II. A clearer view of the workings of our language may enable us to understand better that particular use of words that we call "speaking of God." We shall begin, then, as we must, using words to try to get clear about what goes on in our using words. We shall try to win some clarity about the fact that we *are* linguistic beings, and what follows will be a series of views from several angles of this central fact of our humanity.[1]

Words—what are words? We all know perfectly well what they are, do we not? All we have to do is look (or listen) and see. And when we do, we see that in their natural habitat, words are found in the context of human life. Words are also found isolated from their natural habitat in spelling lists, grammar books, and dictionaries, which serve to teach the agreed use, spelling, and application of words, so that we can go out and use these words in action as others do. Normally, however, words are words-in-action and exist in the context of people doing things together.

People speak, usually to each other. Words are written and read, spoken and heard, in every connection and for every purpose which people make or have. Words used in series according to agreed patterns—language—are woven into the fabric of the whole complex of human life. Words are our tools for living. With words we build roads and houses and bridges.

---

1. Except when I quote or wish to draw attention to the actual words of an author, I shall not, beyond this note, express the indebtedness of what follows to the work of Ludwig Wittgenstein, primarily, and then to that of J. L. Austin, and also to others who have carried forward aspects of their thinking. I acknowledge the debt, and anyone familiar with Wittgenstein's *Philosophical Investigations* will see how vast it is. However, I must take responsibility for making of his thought what I have, and since the description which follows must stand on its own merits, I have refrained as much as possible from referring to the many passages of Wittgenstein's which have led me to these results.

With words we encourage and discourage each other. With words we form and break relationships. Indeed, with these instruments we think and sing and tell stories and love and hate; in short, we live as human beings.

Words may be thought of also as acts. Much conversation, making of promises, writing poetry, and telling stories and jokes are occasions in which the speaking is the doing that we intend. Speaking is a distinctively human way of acting, and it is difficult to imagine human activity without its accompanying language. It is helpful, then, to think of language as behavior, indeed as distinctively human behavior. It is our human way of going about all that we do.

The central role of language in our life is so familiar to us that we do not stop to notice it, but it can be brought into relief by examining what is involved in learning a foreign language. Learning French, for example, is not an insuperable task, first of all because we can speak, read, hear, and write. Not only can we speakers of English do this, but so can the French. We have our language and they have theirs, and both of these languages are used by us in strikingly similar ways. The French do with their language the same things that we do with ours, and the role of French in their life is about what the role of English is in ours. With French words the French build roads and houses, make war and love, engage in politics and business, have riots and holidays, just as we do with our English words. And if we discover that there is a subtle way in which they do these things ever so slightly differently from the way in which we do them, then we have come to the fact that learning a foreign language is more than learning words and grammar from a book: it is also a matter of acquiring a sense of the way of life of the French. To imagine a language in its actual use is to imagine "a form of life,"[2] and to learn a language as it is actually used is to learn to share in a way of life.

The crucial role of language in human life can be noticed again if we reflect on the fact that we have a language and

2. *P.I.*, §19.

animals do not. That is to say, taking *our* language as a model, animals have only partial elements of a language. Their ability to communicate may be used to share a sense of danger, but not a sense that a danger may arise next week. It may be used to call to another, but not to call up memories of past shared experiences. Animals may send each other simple messages, but they cannot tell each other the time of day, stories, or jokes. Animals do not pun, pay each other compliments, tell lies or fairy tales. Some of these differences may have been in his mind when Wittgenstein remarked that if a lion spoke, we should not understand him.[3] The remark warrants reflection.

The picture suggests a lion in his usual jungle or desert setting, perhaps eating some newly killed prey, looking up as we watch from a safe distance, and growling out, "Excuse me for going ahead while this is still fresh." As the lion returns to his dinner, we might well consider whether we had not had a touch too much sun. Was he actually speaking? Do lions have a sense of manners which could account for what, said by a human being, would be an apology? It is hard to say whether we understand or not. The whole situation is so different from our usual cases of understanding and not understanding.

On the other hand, it is not hard to imagine a lion talking as we do, and Lewis Carroll has presented us one in *Through the Looking-Glass*. Alice understands the lion, as well as she understands anyone in Looking-Glass Land, and so do we, but this is a lion who mops his brow from the work of chasing the unicorn all around the town, who stops for tea, who in fact acts as human beings do, including that special way that is speaking. Insofar as animals act as we do, in gesture or expression, we tend to think of them as being human, and insofar as they use sounds and signals to do the sorts of things which we do with words, we tend to say that they have a language. But when we see how few these things actually are and how differently animals act, we begin to see the difference between men and beasts. We get some sense of the point Wittgenstein

3. *P.I.*, p. 223.

was making and we catch a glimpse of how central is language as *we* use it to our whole way of being.

Nothing could be more misleading, then, than to say that language is used for communication. Without language we could hardly live at all! We could not have governments of the sort we have, nor the human relationships we now have. We could not have cities and roads, arguments and friendships, conversation and debate, or books or letters or poetry or science. Behind the superficial remark that without words we could not communicate lies an image of ourselves and our language that is hopelessly inadequate. The image is something like that of two transmitting and receiving stations sending messages to each other. That there is any reason for the messages being sent and received and what we do with them are ignored as irrelevant to language. To say that we speak in order to communicate is to abstract a tiny section of the use of words and call that the whole.

We relate to each other in more ways than with words. Touch, movement and gesture, a smile or a frown—all are important ways in which we "say" things to each other. Many an action "speaks louder than words." Yet none of these gestures or actions would say what they do say were they not embedded in our spoken language. We learn these non-verbal acts along with, and as supplementary to, our learning speech-acts. Indeed some speech-acts, such as saying "Ouch!" are learned as alternatives to instinctive non-verbal acts, such as crying.

We use also our sense of sight with which to make our way in the world. Nevertheless, to say that my eyes tell me that there is a chair over there is a misleading expression. My eyes tell me nothing of the sort. My lips, tongue, and thought tell me all that with words. Of course, I do not usually think of telling myself "what my eyes see," though I might have occasion to tell someone else. Since my infancy, however, others have told me that they see a chair over there, and I have learned from them to use the word "chair" on similar occasions, have learned this so well that I do not have to tell myself what I see

any more, except in unusual circumstances. There can be no
doubt that we discover or experience the world with the help
of our senses, but it is not true that we discover or experience
the world through our senses alone. All that we sense is what
it is for us with and through our speaking of it as we do, as we
have learned to do in learning to speak of what we see, smell,
touch, taste, and hear.

A striking demonstration of the importance of language in
sensory experience can be found in the story of the early
life of Helen Keller, growing up deaf, dumb and blind—
although more than a mere animal—as something less than
fully human, deprived of language and so cut off from full
participation in the world. Without language she could be
savage but neither spiteful nor deceitful. She could be affectionate but not sincere. She could neither lie nor be truthful.
Lacking human language she shared in little of human life.
The remarkable scene, in which she is led to discover not
simply that the wet fluid from the pump goes with certain
movements of her teacher's fingers and other movements of
the lips and throat, but that there is such a thing as a word,
that there are other words, followed by her plunge into
human existence with this discovery, that scene condenses an
experience or series of experiences which for most of us
occurs too early to remember and which has been too well
assimilated to be noticed. That is the experience of learning the
human behavior of using words.

It is tempting to suppose that thinking is logically prior to
language, but this is incorrect. Although we can think without
speaking, I suggest that we cannot think without language.
We think because we speak, and whatever goes on in the heads
of speechless infants, it is not what we have in mind when we
use the word "thinking." It is best to reflect first on the clearest
cases, in which we are reasonably sure that we are entitled to
call a certain case a case of thinking. If we give someone a
problem to solve, and if he asks to have a moment to think
about it and then tells us the answer, we should not hesitate to
call this a case of thinking. We could even ask him to repeat,

out loud, the steps in his thinking, to *tell* us what he had thought. It is not a logical or linguistic blunder to ask a person to *tell* us what he has been thinking, and if he is unable to do so, he should not object to our suggesting that he was not really thinking. We do not need a neurologist to settle the issue. The right use of the word "thinking" is a matter of the right use of language, a question of using this word as we have been trained. This usage shows that thinking depends on language, including thoughts that race faster than we are able to talk. When we cannot say what we are thinking, we use other words or phrases, such as "musing," "daydreaming," "ruminating," and "letting the mind wander."

In other words, we do not first have concepts and then the words for concepts. It would be incorrect to say that Helen Keller first had the concept "water" and then discovered a word to go with the concept. We who have the word can say that she felt the water, but it is difficult to say what the water was for her before she had the word, for our language, with which we settle such puzzles, is designed for usual cases. When we come to unusual cases, we have to stretch our language and come to new agreements about what to say. It is helpful, then, to think of "concept" as another term for "word," for whenever concepts puzzle us, it is words that puzzle us. Indeed, without the word we could not even speak of the concept. Nothing, therefore, is logically prior to, or independent of, language, our agreed pattern of using words.

I do not say that language is ontologically prior, but it is prior in the sense that we learn a language which was in use before we were born. We are trained in the use of an existing language. When we go through this training, therefore, we learn to use words as human beings around us use them, so in learning a language we begin to share in a form of life. The point to be emphasized here is the public character of language, a fact so familiar that we sometimes fail to notice it. Learning to use a language is learning to associate with those who already use that language in all their activities; it is also learning to relate to the world as they do. When I acquire their use of the term "world," their world becomes mine. When I share in their use of the word "fact," their facts become mine. Language is not only the distinctively human way of being in the world, it is also the distinctively social way of being in the world.

Language is a convention. The existence of a language is the mark of an agreement to use certain sounds and symbols in common in a regular way. It therefore marks an agreement in a form of life. This has been expressed by calling language "rule-governed behavior."[4] Learning a language is learning the rules of its use. The child who acquires the word "chair" and uses it at first for tables as well as chairs needs to learn the rule restricting its use to certain objects; for other objects we use other words. Learning a language is mastering the rules of this behavior.

Rules for the use of language are not the same as those found in grammar books, although they are related to them of course. Grammar books give us rules for sentence structure, parts of speech, punctuation, and the like. If we wish to do with language what people around us do, we must follow these grammatical rules, but we must also follow some rules not found in grammar books. One such extra-grammatical rule for the use of the word "thinking," for example, is that it does not apply, as we saw, to the case of a person who cannot say what he is thinking. Attention to such rules, the regularities which obtain in our use of words, helps to prevent misunderstandings of the meaning of words and sentences.[5]

The relationship between using and understanding a word was defined by Wittgenstein in what appears to be a simple equation: "For a *large* class of cases—though not for all—in which we employ the word 'meaning' it can be defined thus:

4. The phrase has been employed extensively by John Searle.
5. Such an investigation has been called "ordinary language philosophy." The clarification of ordinary language is not a study of the most common things people say, nor does it rest on appeal to the use of words "in the street." Ordinary—in the expression "ordinary language philosophy"—means "that which is ordered." Our *ordinary* language is our *conventio-governed* language.

the meaning of a word is its use in the language."[6] If I do not
know the meaning of a word, what I do not know is how to use
the word. When I become clear about how the word is used in
our language, I no longer have any questions about its meaning. Wittgenstein's remark, however, is not quite a simple
equation of meaning and use.

In the first place, there are exceptions to an equation of
"meaning" and "use." The word "meaning" itself has more
than one use. If I had never heard the word "history," I should
probably not understand someone who told me that England
has had a longer history than the United States. On the other
hand, I could learn that use of the word "history" and still say
that I did not know the meaning of history. In this case,
"meaning" is a word related more closely to "importance" than
to "use": I may be asking what we can learn from history or
from the study of history, or I may be asking whether it is
possible and helpful to think of history as "going somewhere"
or "reflecting a purpose," as having significance for, or importance to, us. There is more than one way in which we employ the
word "meaning."

Furthermore, when I am puzzled about the meaning of a
word, Wittgenstein's dictum does not provide me with the
information I want. If I do not know the meaning of a word, I
shall hardly know how to use it. It is therefore no help at all to
tell me to look to the use in order to learn the meaning. Interpreted as a piece of information or as a rule for finding the
meaning of a strange word, Wittgenstein's remark turns out
to be singularly useless.

I think, however, that this dictum can and ought to be
understood in another way. If we take it as a metaphysical
paradox, we can begin to see what Wittgenstein was driving
at: in saying that the meaning of a word is its use in the language, he was inviting us to look at language in a certain way,
namely, when it is being put to work. If we accept that invitation, we shall see that the question of what a word means
includes also a question about the person who uses that word

6. *P.I.*, §43.

and about what he intended in speaking as he did. "Language," in its normal or paradigmatic sense, refers to human language. Understanding language, therefore, means understanding what is going on when people talk. This is the living context of our words.

Failure to attend to the context of words results in a failure to see the context of meaning. This can lead us, when we are trying to understand something, to ask for its essence. For example, in trying to understand religion (the fatal slip has been made already—as if we had ever run into religion in isolation), one might be led to ask for its essence, as distinct from all the particular cases in which we use the word "religion." This, however, is like trying to find the real onion by peeling away all the leaves until nothing is left, whereas it was just the leaves that made up the onion.[7] The mistake is to look for some mysterious entity hidden behind all the actual cases in which we use the word. Once we are clear about what lies before us, however, namely, the actual occasions of our use of the word "religion," what more shall we need? When we get down to the core of an apple, we have the core of an apple, but is that the apple still, much less its "essence"? What we need to understand better is not what we cannot see, but that which is before our eyes.

The open, public, rule-governed features which we have found to be characteristic of our language can assure us that the meanings of words, and all that we need to know in order to understand and use our language, are before our eyes to be seen. There are of course other aspects of language which are not immediately visible and which may be of interest for other reasons, but they tell us nothing about what we actually do with words. For example, each of our words has a history and so an etymology. Historical investigation may tell us about ancient animistic beliefs which lie behind such expressions as "the sun smiles" and "the wind whispering in the trees." Nevertheless, we can learn to use these expressions and

7. Cf. a similar figure in *P.I.*, §164. But an artichoke has a heart, whereas an onion is a flawless illustration of the point.

therefore their meaning without knowing anything at all about such historical findings. Etymology offers no help in learning the meaning of our present language. Again, each word that I speak is undoubtedly accompanied by, or coincides with, physiological or electrical processes in my brain. I need no help from neurologists, however, in order to learn the conventional use of words. Nothing that we need to know about the meaning of our words is hidden from our sight. The wonder and mystery of language, therefore, is right in front of us, if we will but notice and acknowledge it. The mysterious character of a concept, for example, does not lie in its supposed hiddenness. If a concept such as "good" is mysterious, the mystery lies in what we can see and hear and feel, in what human beings do and say to each other with that word. I say that that concept is a word, because they are the same thing. There is nothing denigrating in calling a concept a word, once we acknowledge how important words are in our life. It would be another life indeed if we did not have and use as we do the word "good"!

Some important words seem to contradict the thesis that nothing is hidden, that whatever we need to know to clear up puzzles of understanding lies open to view. Consider the concept—that is, the word—"understanding." Surely, it might be thought, understanding and knowing are strange, hidden, inner processes that go on in the head. But that is a jumble of confusions. No doubt if my head is cut off, I shall be in such a condition that I could no longer be said to understand. Nor do I deny that when I understand what is said, interesting neurological processes go on in my brain. What I am arguing, however, is that when you say that I understand, the word "understand" neither refers to, nor depends for its correct use on any knowledge about, those inner processes. As far as getting clear about the rules for the use of "understanding," "knowing," and "thinking," information about brain cells is of no use whatever. Understanding algebra, for example, is a condition, a state, perhaps, but it is a state of affairs, not an inner, hidden condition. A person can be tested to find out if he understands algebra, and we say he understands when he is able to pass the test. Understanding is the state of having mastered a technique, activity, or material. Whether I have that mastery is decided by what I am able to do and is therefore as open to your judgment as it is to mine. If this were not the case, our whole complex system of testing and examination and critical debate would be other than it is. Our agreement about the potentially public character of knowledge and understanding, that these words are to be used for situations in which others can judge of us better than we, is an important feature of our life. We may not agree in the adequacy of some particular test. We may be of different minds on which testing procedures are appropriate to certain sorts of knowledge, but our agreement that some sort of test is appropriate indicates an important feature of our use of such words as "know," "think," and "understand." It is therefore an important feature of our agreed way of living in the world.[8]

A rule for the use of such words as "think," "know," and "understand" is: look at what you can *see*—and not inside yourself—for the criteria of correct employment. As Wittgenstein put it, "Try not to think of understanding as a 'mental process' at all. For *that* is the expression which confuses you. But ask yourself: in what sort of case, in what kind of circumstances do we say, 'Now I know how to go on . . .'?"[9] The circumstances determine the correct use of these words. To say that to understand is to be able to behave in a certain way (an important part of that behavior being often the act of speaking) is therefore less paradoxical than it may seem at first. This way of putting it brings out the fact that a person's behavior, including his verbal behavior, is the criterion for our saying of him that he understands or knows. Or to put the

8. I take Wittgenstein's argument for the public character of the criteria governing our use of the word "understanding" to be one of his principal contributions to our better grasp not only of the use of that word, but also of the role of our language in our lives.

9. *P.I.*, §156.

point another way, external criteria are generally sufficient for deciding when to say that someone understands.

We have seen that language is characteristically human behavior, through which we experience and relate to objects and each other, and with which we think and understand. Our purpose in this brief examination has been to underscore the fact that in focusing our attention on our language, we are necessarily attending to our whole human existence. Our investigation, however, also leads to the conclusion that language is our peculiarly human way of having and finding our world. Language, therefore, not only provides the tools for considering the problem of religion or any other problem of understanding; it also determines the context in which we seek that understanding.

As we grow from infancy to adulthood, we come to master increasingly complex ways of speaking of the world in all its aspects. In turn this enlargement of language enlarges our world. To learn a new way of speaking of the world is to learn a new way of understanding it, and by the time we are adults we have learned to speak of ourselves and our context in a variety of different ways. There is the way of description, but there is also the way of prescription. It is a fact of our language and life that we do not just describe and make statements about things. We also warn, counsel, recommend, advise, and persuade one another about ways of proceeding in life. Furthermore, we relate ourselves to and discover that world to which we relate ourselves by picturing it in a variety of ways. We use metaphors, for example. We recount our history. We tell stories, sometimes just for entertainment, but sometimes as a way of saying where we find ourselves in life. All these ways of speaking are ways of living in the world.

We must, however, go a step farther: with language we also fashion (or accept from others) the world about us. The only world we have is the one we can speak of. The world is ours, therefore, *as* we speak of it. We use the word 'world,' however, in many different ways, a fact of which the *Oxford English Dictionary* can remind us. We speak of the physical world, the chemical world, the geological world, or the astronomical world. We also speak of the political, the economic, and the historical world. And we have also a psychological world, a personal world, a world of values. Unless we are going to change our language and therewith our form of life, the world will be all these things and more. Our inclination toward consistency will lead us to reject aspects of any of them which do not fit in with the others. Most of us, for example, have decided that the world of demonic forces does not fit the world of the natural and medical sciences well enough to be entertained today. As the world of medicine and psychiatry has grown for us, the world of witches and demons has tended to shrink and disappear. The more we come to speak of the world in the terms of science, the less the world remains what it was for pre-scientific man. The world is what it is for us as we speak of it.

This linguistic determination applies as well to all aspects of our world. The character and quality of facts are determined for us by our way of using the word "fact." We use this word positively or negatively in situations in which our ancestors did not. It occurs to us, for example, to speak of accounts of physical events as factual or non-factual. When we come across stories of ax heads floating in water, for example, or a man walking on water, of the sun standing still, or the seas parting and standing like walls on either side of a path, it strikes us as odd not to use our word "fact" as we use it, subject to the sort of empirical criteria of facticity which mark our use of this word. To our ancestors, the word "fact" did not occur in this connection, nor were they as concerned with empirical criteria.

It might be objected, however, that facts simply are, and that with language we human beings try our best to come to terms with them. Yet even to say this, I have had to use language. Engage as I may in the game of trying to imagine a world without any human being there to speak of it, a world of mere fact, without even the word "fact" with which to speak or think of it, the moment I try to give shape to my inchoate and inarticulate imaginings, I must use words. Facts, William James liked to say, are what we carve our experienced world up into. The idea of a fact-in-itself, a fact "as such," may be seductive, but it depends on a move in thought under the tutelage of the false idea that words are labels for objects. That move forgets that every fact we know is known in, with, and through our way of speaking of it. If there could be a fact-in-itself, a so-called "pure fact," a fact "as such," it would not be of our knowing and we could literally say nothing about it.

This is not at all to deny that there is no world to be experienced and carved up with such a word as "fact." There is, to paraphrase Wittgenstein, all the difference between "fact-behavior" (our speaking of facts) when the relevant facts are present, and the same behavior when the facts are not there.[10] Only, what must also be said is that our descriptions of facts are determined by our language. If we talk about the facts in such a way as to lead ourselves into difficulties, if our way of speaking fails to accomplish our purposes, then a price must be paid, sometimes even with our lives. "That gun is not loaded" is not always the appropriate thing to say. And this is true because of the more basic fact that we have already carved up our experienced world with the word "gun," and with all the other words with which we manufacture, sell, load, and unload such an object.

With language, therefore, we discover and give shape to our whole context and all its parts. How a man speaks of the world reveals the world of which he is speaking. This is only the corollary of the linguistic character of our existence that we have been unfolding. It is worth noting, by way of summary of what has been said so far, that on this linguistic foundation we find ourselves in the same place in which we found the spirit of our times to have directed us: as autonomous pluralists and relativists in a world of change. Now, however, we have given these features of our age a particular focus in our linguistic apprehension of that world. To the extent that we change our ways of speaking, no longer speaking seriously of

10. Cf. *P.I.*, §304.

witches and goblins, for example, we find ourselves in a world different from that of our ancestors. Such a change is the result of choices which we have made (and continue to make) about what to speak of and how. Whatever the subject of our talk, however, it is ours through language, and apart from this relativity there can be nothing to say. Within this relativity, however, there is more than one way to speak. Just this is made evident by religious discourse. Religious discourse, however, must be understood on these foundations as one of a plurality of ways of living linguistically, of being in and having a world as linguistic beings. To an examination of this way we now turn, in beginning to investigate religion within the limits of language alone.

CHAPTER IV

The Problem Restated: The Linguistic Behavior Which Is Religion

If language is our peculiarly human way of living in and having a world, religious discourse must be one way, or an aspect of one way, in which some people are in the world. The proper analysis of religious discourse, then, will consist in a clear description of this way of behaving, comparing it to and contrasting it with other ways, and thereby identifying its linguistic location. Before turning to this task, however, I want to answer some objections which could be made to this way of proceeding. First of all it could be objected that religion cannot be encompassed by language, since religion points to a reality that surpasses language. It could be objected further that the heart of religion, not being a matter of words at all, cannot be adequately described by a linguistic analysis. I wish to expand on, and respond to, these objections first, and then I shall turn to the task of redefining our problem on the foundations of the linguistic character of our human existence which was presented in Chapter III.

I have argued that our language provides us our way of being in, and relating to, a world, which is available to us in, with, and through our language; and that since thinking depends upon language, we cannot conceive of that for which we have no words. In the strictest sense, we do not have to warn ourselves to keep silent about that of which we cannot

61

speak: we have no choice in the matter![1] It might seem, however, that religion is the living refutation of this argument,
being the case par excellence of an experience which surpasses language. After all, is there not sense in the idea of
non-verbal experience? The experience of beauty in nature
or in a work of art may come to mind, or the sense of dread,
awe, or terror during a storm or when we are in physical
danger. Even when we contemplate the limits of our language
and our world, especially when this contemplation happens as
a religious experience, we may feel a sense of mystery and is
this too not an experience of something surpassing language?
And if religion arises from experiences of what surpasses language, then surely it is misguided to constrict religion within
the limits of language alone. Such a Procrustean treatment of
the matter would be inadequate to the subject, since it would
fail to take account of just those features of religious discourse
which we have accused others of ignoring.

This objection depends upon the concept "non-verbal experience." The phrase is used in an attempt to distinguish one
element of our experience, which could also be called "the
immediate impress of things upon us," from a second element,
in which we give some shape to this immediate experience by
forming a concept or using a word.[2] This idea of non-verbal
experience, however, calls for a move in thought logically
similar to that involved in saying that the purpose of language
is communication. A single element in seeing, hearing, or feel-

1. This is not a logical exclusion of all speaking that does not conform
   to the requirements of a system, as we find in *Tractatus*, 7, but a
   tautology. On the similar sounding but radically different point of
   the conclusion of the *Tractatus* (Wittgenstein, *Tractatus Logico-
   Philosophicus* [London: Routledge & Kegan Paul, 1961]), which
   depends on the thesis that only empirical propositions can be sen-
   sibly said, see Max Black in *Essays on Wittgenstein's Tractatus*, ed.
   Copi and Beard (New York: The Macmillan Company, 1966), p.
   102. Cf. E. Stenius, *Wittgenstein's Tractatus* (Oxford: Blackwell,
   1960), pp. 6, 13.
2. Isolation of this "immediate" experience was fundamental to
   Schleiermacher's argument in his *Speeches on Religion*.

ing is isolated from the larger context of our lives, as though what we then went on to do with this pre-verbal and therefore pre-reflective something were no part of the original.

When one reflects upon the pleasure that comes in listening to, let us say, Mozart's *Prague Symphony*, this move in thought seems tempting. We may say that our response is instinctive, but we easily forget that the music to which we respond "instinctively" can seem strange to persons unacquainted with the classics of Western music. Our response has a good deal more training behind it than we may readily recall having acquired. More important, we can obviously say nothing about this non-verbal experience without using words. If we really mean that it is non-verbal, then we cannot talk about it. If, however, we mean only that there is such a thing as listening to and enjoying music without concepts or ideas, without any use of language at the time, then there is no problem. Of course we can do so. But of course, that music was written by someone, was reproduced, sold, purchased, rehearsed, and performed for us by human beings, who without language would hardly be what they are or have done what they did. And if we are going to do anything with this experience, invite others to share it, determine to listen to more Mozart, tell anyone about the performance, or even recall later on the full experience in its context, we shall be using words again. The so-called non-verbal experience is itself imbedded in our linguistic world, for it is the experience of linguistic beings.

I have granted in the preceding chapter that of course we do other things than talk, but if we did not have language, who can say (!) what these other things would be? Our experiences which do not involve the use of words are unconnected with the rest of our lives unless we say something, even if *what* we say is that we cannot find words adequate to those experiences.

I am not arguing the absurd position that pain-behavior, such as saying "Ouch!" is the same as having a pain, nor that hearing a piece of music is the same thing as talking about it afterward. I am saying, however, that the experiences of pain, of hearing a piece of music, of seeing a landscape or a painting, are human experiences which have their place *within* the context of our linguistic apprehension of the world. It is characteristic of some experiences which we linguistic beings have to say we cannot find words adequate to them. The tendency to say this is, however, often in inverse proportion to our training in speaking about the matter at hand, for we often appreciate a work of art better after hearing a lecture or reading a book about it by a connoisseur. And even faith comes by hearing, as we have been told, for which prophets and preachers are necessary. We shall return to this matter later, but perhaps enough has been said here to meet one objection to investigating religion within the framework of our linguistic existence.

It could still be objected, however, that language is not of the essence of religious faith, that faith is other than language, an emotion, perhaps, and that consequently an understanding of the language associated with religion would not bring understanding of the religion itself. Religious faith, it can be argued, is like human love, in that when we have understood all that can be said about love, we still have not understood love if we have not loved. This argument makes a valid and important distinction: there is a difference between understanding love, in the sense of knowing how to identify it when we run into it, and the state that we call being in love. Using "understanding" in a participatory sense, we can say that only the lover understands love. Nevertheless, we identify the world's great lovers by their writings, which reminds us that it is as linguistic beings that we love and are loved, and were we not linguistic beings, human relationships of all sorts would be quite other than they are. In both senses of understanding, therefore, understanding love depends upon using the language *of* love and the language *about* love. In order to love or to understand love in a fully human way, language is indeed necessary.

Is this also true of religion? Friedrich Waismann reported that Wittgenstein once said to him, "Is speech essential for

religion? I can quite well imagine a religion in which there are
no doctrines, and hence nothing is said. Obviously the essence
of religion can have nothing to do with the fact that speech
occurs—or rather: if speech does occur, this itself is a component of religious behavior and not a theory. Therefore
nothing turns on whether the words are true, false, or nonsensical."[3] These remarks date from a period in Wittgenstein's
life when he thought that the only linguistic act worthy of
attention was that of making statements which could be true
or false. Consequently, he could say that if there were no
doctrines, no *theories* in a religion, then *nothing* was being said.
This conception of language, however, was repudiated by him
by the time he wrote the *Philosophical Investigations*, for there,
as I have argued, he has shown through example piled on
example that we are who and what we are in and with our
words, that language is our distinctively human way of being
in and apprehending our world. Language is so central to our
behavior that it is a pointless if not impossible task to imagine
religious or any other behavior as it might be apart from our
speaking. We shall therefore make the most of what may be
taken as the positive side of Wittgenstein's remark, interpreting religious discourse as a decisive component of religious
behavior.

I do not deny for a moment that we have other senses than
those employed in using language, or that we do things without using words. I do not deny that we do some things for
which we have no words. Wittgenstein's example is as good as
any: "Describe the aroma of coffee—Why can't it be done? Do
we lack the words?"[4] There, we might say, is a clear case of a
non-verbal experience. If we consider the case, however, we
shall see that this conclusion is mistaken.

Why can we not describe the aroma of coffee? The answer is
simple and obvious: we have no need to. We have noses with
which to smell the aroma of coffee and distinguish it from other

3. F. Waismann, "Notes on Talks with Wittgenstein," *The Philosophical Review*, LXXIV (1965), 16.
4. *P.I.*, §610.

smells well enough for our purposes. The phrase "the aroma of coffee" is therefore all the description we need, coffee being common enough in our world for this aroma to be familiar to most of us. Smelling is smelling, and seeing is seeing, and we linguistic beings do both. Where language comes in is at the point at which we do something with what we smell and see, as when we ask for a cup of coffee, or tell someone what we have seen. "The aroma of coffee" being the adequate description of that aroma, the smell of coffee is not an example of non-verbal experience. Although we have no further descriptions for certain smells, feelings, and sights than our references to them, these experiences are not beyond language.

But surely, it might be further objected, we are aware of aspects of the world which surpass language? Surely we have experiences which cannot be grasped with words. Does not this show that *what* we experience is prior to language? I do not dispute such an awareness or such experiences, but I question the conclusion. It rests on too narrow a view of our language, as if only precise description, fit for computer programming perhaps, were all that could properly be called language. We are not computers, however. We are human beings who also write poetry, speak in metaphors, make points indirectly, hint, suggest, and talk around the subject. For example, speaking of love as being more than we can ever say is a way of speaking which shows that love is not the same as the dimensions of a piece of wood. When human beings love, they do so as linguistic beings, and so they find it appropriate to say certain things as part of that behavior which we call loving. And a clear way in which to see that that behavior is different from the behavior of giving the measurements of a block of wood is to notice that we write poems of love, for example, or say that our words are inadequate—and we do neither when we give measurements. Human love is characterized by our way of speaking of it.

We conclude, therefore, that in a strict sense there are no non-verbal experiences, if by that is meant experiences about which nothing at all is or can be said. If there were, nothing at all *would* be said about them, not even that nothing can be said about them! That we have experiences which we cannot describe is not denied, but description is not the only use of language. If, therefore, we reckon within only that of which we can speak, we are not omitting anything of which something could be said, which is very close to saying we are not leaving *anything* out. This applies to those experiences of which we say that they are indescribable or that they are not exhausted in words.

When we turn from these considerations of language to the particular uses which we meet in religion, our proposal to understand religion as linguistic behavior receives further confirmation. Had Wittgenstein claimed that religion consists of more than doctrines understood (or rather, misunderstood) as theories, we should not have objected. Praying, singing, meeting together, meditating, making moral decisions are all part of many or most forms of Christianity, and many of those activities appear in other religious traditions as well. Religions are practices as well as traditions, and the traditions are more than just doctrinal. However, if it were further claimed that religion consists of more than can be said, that claim could not be supported, for if there were some "more," and if that "more" could not be spoken of, then nothing whatsoever would be said of it, not even that it is a "more" beyond speech. It seems reasonable, then, to begin by saying that whatever can be said about religion will be said in human words, that here too language is our principal tool for understanding a religion.

I wish, however, to make a larger claim than that. I want to claim that it makes sense to attempt to understand a religion such as Christianity, in any of its various forms, as a linguistic enterprise, and that when we try to understand religion as linguistic behavior, we are entering the subject by the front door, not crawling in a basement window. It is well to remind ourselves once more that to say that a religion is a linguistic enterprise is not to say that it consists simply and exclusively in talk. It will indeed include talk, but *human* talk, human language used to do the things that we associate with religion,

including thinking, meditating, reflecting, wondering, rejoic-
ing, forgiving, loving, deciding, and much more. If we can
understand what is going on in the language-in-use in what we
call a religion, we shall have understood all that can be understood of that religion.

When we consider the historical origins and development of
Christianity, we find that Christians have always acknowledged
the centrality of language in their religion. They have paid
the highest respect to a book, or to the story or stories con-
tained in that book, regarding as of the utmost importance how
they themselves spoke of matters of which its authors wrote.
They have consequently considered as crucial what men say
to each other and what they do to each other with their
words, e.g., bearing false witness or breaking a promise. It has
been further held by Christians that they were men and women
who had heard and remembered a message, word, or story,
and that they owed it to each other to remind each other of that
message or story. It is true that Christianity has been primarily
a way of life, but it has generally been held to be the way of
life of those who have heard the biblical story and who are
open to hearing it again and again. Faith comes by hearing,
the apostle Paul wrote, and hearing the story of Israel, its
promise and its hope, and taking up that story and making it
one's own, as we might say, has been at the heart of the
Christian's way of life. Christianity, then, seems to confirm
our proposed method of investigation. In its Scriptures, its
many historical expressions, its cultic activity, and its dogmas
and teachings from various times, it has put language in the
center of the picture it presents.[5]

The doctrinal canons of various ecumenical councils of
fourth- and fifth-century Christianity offer an illustration of
the importance of language in this religion. In addition to
defining what should be said by believers, these councils

5. I have developed this point at greater length in "On Doing Theology," in *Talk of God*, ed. G. N. A. Vesey, Royal Institute of
Philosophy Series, Vol. II (London: Macmillan and Co., 1969), pp.
52–71.

added a list of sentences which Christians were told *not* to say—e.g., that Christ had one nature—for if anyone were to say such a thing, so each item concludes, *anathema sit*. Literally, that is, whoever says such a thing is thereby cast out, cut off from the Christian community. Put in more sympathetic terms, he who speaks in this other way is no longer speaking as Christians do and puts himself outside of this linguistic community. To be part of this community is to talk in a certain way, to say some things and not others, and this fact attests to the fundamentally linguistic character of the Christian community. We make no mistake, then, in describing this religion as linguistic activity. To understand the workings of religious discourse, consequently, is to understand religion.

The example of the conciliar *anathema sit* shows that Christians have understood that when we exclude a certain way of speaking, we exclude a certain way of living, and also rule something out of our world. Most of us in the West, for example, have ruled out speaking of witchcraft and black magic as explanations for human behavior or physical occurrences. We have replaced them as explanations by the notions of mass hysteria and using various other psychological states. To this extent, we live in a world more naturalistic than that of our ancestors. We *could* also decide to limit our world to what may be spoken of in the terms of the physical sciences; in fact, however this further step would be difficult for us to carry out, for, as Wittgenstein observed, some of our most common and important words ("I," for example) are not characteristic of physics. To imagine a world in which personal pronouns, proper names, and our common words for human relationships were no longer used is to imagine a form of life strikingly different from our own. Decisions about language are decisions about life, and changing our ways of speaking changes our way of life.

In order to achieve an adequate analysis of religious discourse, it is essential to remember the intimate relationship between language and life which our Western religious traditions confirm. If we recall that relationship, religious discourse will be seen as human behavior, a particular way of life. Consequently, whether to use the word 'God' as the religious man does is a question about how to situate oneself in the world, and about the sort of world to which one is related. This accounts for the fact that conversion, either to or from a religious position, has usually been regarded as a change of a person's whole way of life. This is the change about which we have to become clear if we wish to be clear about the word 'God' as a characteristic feature of religious discourse.

'God,' then, is not a separate, discrete concept or word for investigation, for any who wish to understand religious discourse. To examine the word in isolation from its context in the life of religious people is to pursue an abstraction. 'God' as a discrete concept regardless of context is simply not the same word 'God' that occurs in religious discourse. In religious discourse, this word is at the center of a complex linguistic pattern and the role it plays is related to everything else that the religious person wants to say.

A striking example of this occurs in a scene in Dostoevsky's *Crime and Punishment*, in which Raskolnikov, pressing Sonya, draws from her how near to the limits of human endurance she has come, how humanly hopeless is the situation in which she finds herself.[6] When Sonya feebly but resolutely insists that God will protect her, Raskolnikov persists in his cynical questioning until she can say nothing. Finally, when asked sarcastically what God ever does for her in response to her prayers, Sonya, after a long silence, finally manages to whisper: "He does everything!" Her reticence and her inability to respond, continuing as the scene develops, bring Raskolnikov to see at least this much about Sonya the believer: "how difficult it was for her to expose and betray all that was *her own*." "Her own!" "Everything!" For the believer, insofar as he is a believer, everything does depend upon God. To put this point linguistically, 'God' is the word which stands inseparably in the

6. Dostoevsky, *Crime and Punishment*, trans. Jessie Coulson (London: Oxford University Press, 1953).

center of, and related to, every other feature of that linguistic
activity to which we refer with the phrase "religious discourse."
Abstracted from that context, the word 'God' no longer
performs the function which we want to understand.

The history of Christian theology supports the contention
that 'God' has to be understood in relationship to the whole
context of what Christians have to say, the word 'theology'
("God-talk") covering the whole range of doctrine and its
elaboration. It has been characteristic of theology to argue
that no part of its subject matter is independent of what is said
in that part of theology which explicitly develops a doctrine
of God. Consequently, it has been held that only the whole
of theology unfolds the meaning of the concept 'God'. As
theology became more systematic, from the time of the Scholas-
tics, through that of the sixteenth-century Reformers, to
modern times, this feature became increasingly explicit.
Whether every theologian succeeded in connecting all points
of his systems with the center, his intention of doing so was
explicit.

Consequently, if 'God' is the key term about which we
want to be clear, we have to understand how this word is used
by a contemporary Christian, embedded in the whole linguistic
activity of religion. Therefore, to set up a minimal definition
of God and seek to examine *that*, as we have seen happen in
the factual interpretation of religious discourse, is a move
doomed to failure. A conclusion reached by examining this
minimally defined term will not help us understand the word
in its proper context, for in that context the term is not used
as minimally defined. Indeed, we approach the actual problem
only if we ask, not about a minimally defined God, but about
the triune God of which the Christian speaks. The believer
will insist that the word is being used in a way quite different
from the way he intends if it is not connected with speaking of
both Jesus of Nazareth and the Spirit. The doctrine of the
Trinity has generally been held to be primary or fundamental,
not a composite doctrine that might or might not have been
put together. It is a starting place for, and not a conclusion to,

reflection about God. Furthermore, talk of a triune God is itself derived from the biblical writings and it is said to be their inescapable corollary. The context in which the Christian's use of the word 'God' is to be placed, then, is the biblical material and the later doctrine thought to be consistent with those writings.

Finally, the believer's use of the word 'God' occurs in the context of, and is itself an important part of, his living in this world as he thinks a Christian ought to live. If our aim is to clarify the religious discourse of the educated Christian today, we must see the word 'God' as the central term of this whole context. Our task, then, is to describe the linguistic behavior of a man who speaks in this way in this context. Only such a description can provide an adequate analysis of religious discourse.

Much of what has aimed at the analysis of religious discourse has not pursued this task. Analysts have tried instead to understand an abstraction from language. Christian talk about God, so begins the abstracting process, is of the self-revealing God, the God of the biblical authors. It is talk about the God who has acted and still acts in the world. It is then asked: Just what is this God who acts and speaks? For, unless we can make sense out of this, what sense can be made of religion at all? Surely, it has been said, Christianity stands and falls with its doctrine of God, and so the focus has been placed on the concept of God defined by that doctrine.

This line of abstraction, leading to an examination of the word 'God' in isolation from its context in the linguistic behavior of believers ends by finding the concept incoherent. So analyzed, it *is* incoherent, and we can only regret that analysts have given so little attention to the fact that—as we shall show later on—Christians have said this themselves from the beginning.

Nevertheless, there have been and still are Christians who have tried to defend the coherence of this concept of God; they may be designated as biblical or doctrinal literalists. Like the skeptical analysts, they have thought it essential to Christianity to defend the coherence of speaking of God in this abstracted fashion. The difficulty with the position can be demonstrated briefly by considering what sense could be made, on the linguistic grounds considered, of the concept of a God who speaks, a God whose word is supposed to have been addressed to, and heard by, human beings. Let us develop the alternatives already mentioned.

The God under consideration, we recall, is the "minimally defined" God of a theism abstracted from the language of Christians and defended by believers of a literalistic turn of mind. This God is by definition utterly unlike any human being, far more different, indeed, from anything else we experience, since everything that we experience is a part of creation, whereas God is its creator. But if such an "other" God were to speak, how could we understand him and be able to say that he had spoken? If we could not understand a lion that talked, how much less could we understand a God who talked? If we could not know the role that talking played in the lives of gods, how could we know that what God had done was a case of speaking? Whatever God's language might be, if God is utterly other than we are, how could we begin to understand this divine language? We are confronted by a far greater problem than that of translation, for even the minimum conditions which (as we have shown in the previous chapter) make translation a possibility, are not present. We simply do not know if divine language is for a divine being what human language is for us.

It might be thought, however, that when God speaks to man, he causes by some miracle at least some men to understand him as they understand other men. But this idea gets us no further than the first attempt. It is only a circuitous form of the previous alternative, for appeal to a miracle of understanding excludes giving any account whatsoever of the use of the word "understand" in this claim. To "understand-by-a-miracle" would be to do something so unlike anything we call "understand," that we could not distinguish it from "not understanding." Since the rules for its use are not available, there is no way in which to know how to use the expression "to understand-by-a-miracle." If a religious community were to make up its own rules for the use of this expression, it would hardly be any easier for any member of *that* community to show a relationship between those rules and our conventions for the use of the word "understand." So if it is said that a God wholly unlike us has spoken, and that, by a miracle, someone has heard and understood that God, there is no way in which to settle this claim, or even to understand what is being claimed. The expression remains unrelated to the roles which understanding and not understanding play in our language.

If, as Tillich has said, God is so unlike us as to be not a being at all, but the ground of all being, then of course it (or he) would hardly engage in such a human activity as speaking. Consequently, there could be no question of understanding the word of such a God, since there would be no word to understand.

Contrariwise, if a move is made in the other direction, toward a God who is very much like us, then talk about understanding a divine word begins to make sense, but only at a considerable price. A God of whom it is claimed that he spoke and was heard and understood by a man in a way conforming to the rules of our language, and thus who spoke our language, would have to be a most human sort of God. He would have to do much of what we human beings do with language, and language would have to be the same for him as it is for us. Such a God, for example, would not know what we were thinking unless we told him or unless he spied on us. Such a God could speak a creative word, let us say, but it would be creative only in the same way in which human words are sometimes creative, though perhaps more frequently. A speaking God who could be understood by men, then, would be more than figuratively anthropomorphic. He could hardly be the God of doctrinally literalistic theism.

It should be quite clear that no educated Christian, as we have defined him, is going to believe in the minimally defined

God of doctrinally literalistic theism. In other words, reflecting our linguistic considerations, the contemporary educated
Christian will not use the word "God" in that way. The
behavior that has been explored in these alternatives and
shown to be absurd is simply not the behavior which we have
set out to understand, in spite of the fact that many of the
critics of Christianity would like to have it otherwise. For the
Christian who is aware of the culture of which he is a part,
using the word 'God' is itself part of a more complex linguistic behavior, and that behavior is not being examined at
all in such a minimal investigation.

Consider some of the features of the use of the word 'God'
as it has been used by Christians. 'God' appears at first glance
to be a proper name, yet this "person" is not only never seen:
he is distinguished primarily by his *absence*. He is, furthermore, the central figure in a complex literature, the Bible,
having a certain dramatic narrative structure. This story (or,
simply, the Bible, since the whole complex of biblical writings
form only in a loose sense a single story) is considered by the
religious man as basic to his use of the word 'God.' The story
of this 'God' is of one who has a proper name indeed, but a
name that is not to be pronounced. This largely absent "person," with a name not to be used, is mentioned largely by
circumlocution: the biblical writers appear to have wanted
to talk around their subject, rather than to come at it directly.
In these writings, furthermore, there is a story of God's com-
manding that no image be made of him. We are given, then, a
largely absent presence, an unmentionable name of what is
neither to be imagined, nor pictured, nor otherwise rep-
resented! And not only is this God thus not an object, or a
person, or even an idea, but faithfulness to this God is
measured by how a man lives and walks ahead in life. Faithfulness to this God consists in living by law, not in developing
some inner state. The central place of the Law in the biblical
story stands as a protest to the rationalistic interpretation of
religion which minimally defined and doctrinally literalistic
theism presents. The Law stands as the Bible's warnings not

to think of believing as a "mental process." Believing in this God is in no way like believing a statement to be true or even like thinking of a concept. "Believing," being faithful, is first of all a matter of behaving in certain ways, walking ahead with a certain lamp to guide one's feet.

Finally, whatever he is, this God is not a finished, fixed, or identifiable figure, person, or concept. The biblical God is a God of the future, a future coming to meet men. He does not belong to a past to contemplate, and the present tense seems to have little to do with a God of whom the story says that he *will* be "all in all" (whatever that may mean). This absent presence, this unnameable one, this unimaginable "you" gives men a way to walk and waits somewhere out ahead of man. These are only some of the features of the way in which the word 'God' is used that we must remember if we wish to analyze contemporary religious discourse adequately.

The question is this: What is the contemporary Christian doing when he uses the word 'God' as he does? This speaking in riddles and paradoxes, this taking back what is said as soon as it is said, though refusing to give up using the word, what sort of linguistic placing can this be given? In a word, what account can we give of such linguistic behavior?

In order to answer this question, it will be necessary to consider a form of linguistic behavior which has not received attention, and which holds promise of showing what it is that is happening when a contemporary, educated Christian speaks of God. This behavior lies along what I shall call the edges of our language. The first step toward an answer to our question, therefore, will draw attention to, and clarify the idea of, the edges of language. The second step will clarify, in the light of our earlier reflections on language, the linguistic behavior of speaking at the edges of language, beginning first with some patterns of behavior more or less closely related to that of religion, and then discussing those directly associated with the Christian religion. Once this behavior is clear, the third step will show that this analysis of religious discourse produces a more adequate description than those which present it as a set of factual propositions, as the expression of a moral commitment, or as a metaphysical proposal. We shall conclude by pointing out what sort of issue is posed for a contemporary man confronted by the choice between religion and irreligion.

CHAPTER V
The Edges of Language

Language has limits. We cannot put words together in any way we please and still be speaking a language. To say "This not ever but" is to not to engage in what we call speaking. Each of those four words is a perfectly good word, but we do not put them together that way. Consequently, strung together like this they say nothing at all. Merely putting words together grammatically, however, is not enough in order to engage in language. If someone greets me with "Good morning," and I reply, "I did not," I have not made an understandable response, although I have violated no rule of grammar. My reply was a violation of our rules of use, and these rules are of the essence of language. To say that language has limits, then, is another way of saying that language is rule-governed behavior. If we subtract the working of rules from the activity of language, we no longer have language. To dispense with the rules of use is to dispense with language.

Language has limits because its rules cover specifiable ranges of application. Rules are conventions, agreements to use words in certain circumstances and for certain purposes, and by their definition they restrict us. "You're welcome" is a response to make when thanked, but it is limited to that and will not do as a response when someone asks us the time of day. Each part of our language has such restrictions. It is therefore analytically true, true by definition, that language as rule-governed behavior has limits.

The point, however, is not simply one of definition. It is an identifiable feature of our language that it works by rules which govern the employment of its words and expressions. To use an example of Wittgenstein's, "A dog cannot be a hypocrite, but neither can he be sincere,"[1] The rules for the use of the word "hypocrite" and the word "sincere" limit their use to beings which talk. Dogs and trees are therefore not things for which these words are used. *That* such limits exist and *where* they exist can be found out by examining our language in operation.

The rules of our language are not *logically* necessary, nor is there a logical necessity to the limits occurring where they do. The rules of language could conceivably be different from what they are. Actually to conceive of such alternatives, however, is difficult; we are so accustomed to living and speaking as we do that it requires a science-fiction imagination to think up other ways in which language might work, since in order to do so, we have also to think up quite other ways in which life might be lived. If we imagined a way of speaking, for example, that made no distinction between acting a part on a theatre stage and the rest of our activity, we should have to exclude from that imagined way of life any discussion about whether "all the world's a stage," for there would be no alternative.

"If someone says, 'if our language had not this grammar, it could not express these facts'—it should be asked what 'could' means here."[2] The point of this remark of Wittgenstein's is that if our language worked differently, it simply *would* not express the same facts. It is a matter of fact, not a matter of logical necessity, that our language works as it does. It just is the case that we distinguish as we do between fact and fancy, between what exists and what does not (although we do this in a number of different ways). One might imagine another language in which such words as "appear" and "disappear," "exist" and "not exist," "think" and "not think" worked according to quite different rules from those that we

1. *P.I.*, p. 229.   2. *P.I.*, §497.

follow. If the rules were different, the limits of their application would differ as well. In some imaginable language, for example, it could be in order to apply the words "hypocrite" and "sincere" to dogs as well as to people. With that shift from our rules of language would go necessarily a shift in how people lived with dogs, as well as a shift away from our present requirement that what a person *says* will determine whether we call him one or the other. If the rules for the use of these words were extended to cover trees and flowers as well, then again the way in which such a people lived with nature would be different from ours. In short, men could conceivably come to other agreements in the use of words, and so the range of application of their words could be other than is currently the case. But since in point of fact our language works as it does and not otherwise, it has the rules we follow. That means that for any word or expression, the rules for its use permit us to go so far and not further. Our language, as rule-governed behavior, has limits.

There is of course a sense in which our language is at least theoretically unlimited. Not only do we invent new words, but from time to time we change the rules for the use of our words as we find new things to do with language. In the natural sciences, engineering, and technology, discoveries of new activities or phenomena lead frequently to changes of language, made sometimes by inventing new words, sometimes by grouping older words in new combinations, such as "blast-off" and "count-down." Special effects are also produced by combining older and newer uses of a word, as in a delicious advertisement for a houseboat in *The New York Times* a few years ago, which, after pointing out what a satisfactory solution this boat provided to the housing problem in the city, concluded with the claim: "This pad really rocks!"

The fluidity of language and therefore of the limits of its use is evident in the dictionary qualifications, *archaic* and *colloquial*, the one signaling a use passing out of our language, a rule followed decreasingly, the other a new use only beginning to be widely accepted. A shift in the rules is taking place, and this is often a shift in the limits within which a particular word or expression does its work. These conventions in the use of words enable human beings to do an almost endless number of things, and when they decide to do new and different things, they are able to change their language for these new purposes. Yet at any particular time there are limits to what we can do with words, limits to the conventions that give a particular society its character; and these conventions of language, just because they are conventions, reach as far as they do and not further. There comes a point beyond which words no longer do their work.

There are at least two difficulties in conceiving of the limits of language, one unavoidable and one avoidable. The unavoidable difficulty is that we live and think within the framework of language which we wish to comprehend. There is no way in which we can lift ourselves out of our linguistic existence and survey the scene from some superior vantage point; we are unavoidably within the circle of language that we wish to understand. Consequently, we have difficulty thinking of the limits of that beyond which we cannot go and for which, by definition, we have no words.[3] We have no choice but to remain within language and from there attempt to get clear about the fact of its limits. Any discussion of our language must necessarily be conducted by means of language.

Reflection on language's limits as those within which we must do our thinking, however, is a more difficult task than it need be, if we make the avoidable mistake of regarding language as a cage which restricts our freedom of movement.

3. To argue that we might go beyond language by means of *intuition*, or that by intuition we might know something which lies beyond language and is more than can be said with words, is to misunderstand our use of the word "intuition." We use that word for cases in which we know—or think we know—something, but cannot say how we have come by this knowledge. Intuition can go as far as knowledge, but it suffers the defect of being unable to give an account of how it got there. It can certainly not take us farther than language. Hence Wittgenstein's note (*P.I.*, §213): "Intuition an unnecessary shuffle." (Cf. *P.I.*, §214).

That is a picture of language which is neither helpful nor necessary. Worse, if we are captivated by this picture of language as a cage, we misunderstand the role which language plays in our lives. Indeed, the picture is itself a product of misunderstanding the role of our language. It assumes that we can conceive of an inside and an outside of this cage, perhaps even that we stand apart from the cage and see it holding humanity captive. This assumption, however, depends upon forgetting the fact that we are already making use of language in doing this imagining, and are therefore never outside language. The bird-cage picture of language is not true to the role which language actually plays.

It may be that the word "limit" is causing the trouble, presenting the picture of a line that marks off one area within the limit from another area beyond it, which we can see just as well. In order to break away from these inadequate models of language, it may be helpful to present a rather different picture, as different, for example, as the role of the walls in a squash court and that of the outer lines on a tennis court. In squash, unlike tennis, there is no "out," no possibility of marking the fall of the ball beyond the boundaries of the court, since in squash the ball is played against the walls and may bounce off any or all of them. So it is with our language. Language works up to the limits of our conventions, and then it does not work at all.

To counteract the picture of a cage, we might employ a picture of a platform on which to stand as a model for thinking of the role of language. On this platform we can move around, walk or dance or sleep, indeed do all the things we do together with words. Far from imprisoning us, it gives us freedom. The planks of this platform are the rules for use of words, and the planks are of various but determinate lengths. They stick out, as it were, only so far. If we wish to extend this platform, then we must build it out while standing on it. Language serves as the base on which we may stand in order to extend that base, and it is also (to mix our metaphors) the hammer and nails with which an extension to any plank must be secured.

Moreover, the planks, being matters of convention, can be added on only by the joint efforts of many others, for an extension of language must be a social act, just as language itself is. An extension is an agreement on a further use by the users of the language. Nailing on new planks or extensions to old planks, then, is the work of many hands.

Using this picture, we may speak better of the edges of language rather than of its limits. We can go so far out on the platform of language, but if we try to go further, we fall off into a misuse of words, into nonsensical jabbering, into the void where the rules give out. We can, if we are so inclined, walk right along the edge of language, or stand teetering on one place on its circumference. We can, on the other hand, find this a silly place to stand and choose to confine our life to the no-nonsense areas as well within the edges of language, where the rules are clear, their application is undisputed, and language is safely unproblematic.

The safe, central area of language is the part we know best, where we are so familiar with the rules that misunderstandings hardly ever occur. Or to put it another way, here is where the rules work so well that we scarcely notice them. Where we begin to wonder about how to use a word, or whether the rules we have been following will allow us to go a step further, there we are coming to the edges of language. We are approaching the point at which language breaks down, where it ceases to be language because we can no longer do anything with it.

Our suggestion of language as a platform, however, is only a picture. Although it may help us to break loose from the image of a cage, it is too simple to be adequate to the complexity of the full range of our language. Let us abandon pictures, then, and turn instead to actual cases, for in the examination of actual uses of words, the feature of our language to which I wish to draw attention can best be displayed.

The feature of our language which I want to describe is connected with the fact that we sometimes extend the application of words, stretching their use from the range within which they work straight forwardly, out into areas in which they work less clearly. A word works least ambiguously on what I shall call its home-field.[4] The rules for its use on that field permit us, however, to set the word to work in other fields in what we call a figurative way. To this stretching, however, there is a limit, not always sharp, beyond which we are unable to use the word and still be understood, and beyond which we ourselves cannot account for what we are doing with the word. Beyond some point, the use of the word becomes extraordinary, no longer rule-governed or ordinary (in the sense of "ordered by our conventions"). I wish to concentrate attention on the employment of words just short of this total break with the rules for their use. I shall speak of this employment as lying along "the edges of language," an employment to be made clear by examining actual cases.

Let us begin with our usual talk about common physical objects. (Our language is so rich in this area that we cannot pretend to be exhaustive, not even in the limited examples which we shall choose. Our aim is not to say all that can be said, but only to bring out certain aspects of this talk.) We may begin with the case of calling something solid—a piece of rock, for example. In common life, nothing can be less ambiguous than calling a rock solid. "Solid as a rock," we say. But we extend the use of this expression to speak of more complex objects, such as a building. We say of a building that it is solid as a rock. More figuratively yet, we can say that an argument is solid. By that we mean that it will stand up to critical examination, that it will not fall to pieces when attacked. Furthermore, we can say that Jones is solid, which is to say that he is steady, can be relied upon. Institutions can also be called solid, whether we are speaking of financial institutions, such as banks, or political institutions, such as governments. We also speak of a solid majority, or of a political unit, such as a town or a county, as being solidly of one

4. Ian Crombie used the metaphor of a word "playing on its Home Ground" and "playing away" (*New Essays in Philosophical Theology*, ed. Flew and MacIntyre [London: S.C.M. Press, 1955], p. 111).

political party or another. The extension of the word "solid" goes far afield.

Yet the range is not infinite. We come to uses where we must stop and ask whether we still know what we are doing. Can we say that a country is solid? Stable, yes; but it is not clear without further elaboration what it would mean for a country to be solid; this application of the word is evidently less clear than in the case of saying that a bank is solid, or that Jones is solid. Or again, if someone said that the world is solid, I should be puzzled. Since the issue is not clear, I have difficulty imagining the opposite. A rock that is not solid is not to be depended on when rock climbing. A business that is not solid is not one to invest in. But a world that isn't solid? When the issue becomes difficult to grasp, so does the use of the word. The use of the word goes far, but not infinitely far. For the word "solid" the edge lies just beyond speaking of persons and institutions. To call the world, or history, or the universe solid is to drop off that edge, right out of our language altogether.

Another way in which we speak of objects is by describing their texture as rough or smooth. The surface of an object can be rough or smooth, and of course the one shades off into the other, giving us a wide range of different degrees of roughness and smoothness. There is little or no ambiguity in speaking of a rough road, or a smooth cliff, though the criteria in each case are different. But we speak not only of a rough road. We extend the word so that we can speak of a rough ride, which may result from traveling a rough road, but may also be due to a badly sprung vehicle. The use of the word extends further and permits us to speak of a rough remark, which can be unsettling or shake us emotionally and need by no means be made in a rough voice. A rough remark can be made in quite a smooth voice!

The convention-controlled use of this term, however, lets us move with it in other directions. We can speak of a rough period of history, or a rough period in a person's life, when "things" are not going smoothly. We can also speak of a rough character, or, which is surely not the opposite, of someone being a bit too smooth. Yet here we are coming near the edge. A piece of writing may be rough, that is, unfinished, not polished, but can we say that the ideas in a rough draft are rough? Are ideas either rough or smooth? Their expression, yes, but it is not so clear what it is to have rough ideas, although we can have a rough idea of what someone wants to say.

A government, or its agent the police, may be rough with the people, but it is not clear what it would mean to call a country rough, unless we were speaking of the terrain or the conditions of life there. And is red rougher than blue? If a period of time has been rough, could we say that all of history is rough? Apparently not. Roughness being a relative term, we need to have a point of comparison, which limits our use of these terms to what can be thought of as parts, or examples, but the distinction hardly works when everything is being referred to. Here too we have edges of doubt and then confusion, a gradual limit to the areas into which the use of these words can be stretched.

These examples of our talk of objects may serve to introduce an examination of other ranges of language which will prove more fruitful for our study. We shall consider first several cases in the biological realm, and then turn to some more important ways in which we speak of ourselves. When we turn from speaking of physical objects to our talk about biological phenomena, we do not pretend that biological entities are not also physical objects. Nonetheless, when we speak of things which are alive, we make use of certain words whose home-field is our talk of animate creatures and which we are extending when we apply them to what is inanimate. Likewise, when we turn later on to some of the ways in which we speak of ourselves, especially when speaking of our minds, we shall not be assuming that there can be talk about mind when there cannot also be talk about a brain. Nevertheless, "brain" and "mind" are words at home in different fields. Unlike "brain," "mind" is a word which is not used to refer to an object. On this field in which "mind" is at home, we come across a whole range of words whose use must be stretched in order to apply them to anything other than human beings. The distinctions which we are following, then, between inanimate objects, animate beings, and human persons, is not intended to reflect a progression, say, from lower to higher, or even from less complex to more complex, but only reflects a difference between them that is an important part of our language and therefore of the way in which we situate ourselves in a world of objects, living organisms, and persons.

Living organisms grow, we say. A plant grows, a dog grows, a child grows. Growth is a concept at home in the field of the animate. Yet we have agreed to extend the word into other realms as well. We speak of a city growing, perhaps because the expansion of population and building is the product of the energies of the city itself, or more literally, of the people in that city. The lack of this inner energy may also account for the fact that we do not ordinarily think of a building under construction as growing, nor do we usually apply this word to a piece of machinery, such as an automobile, being assembled part by part on a production line. We do speak of a nation growing, and so of younger and older nations. We also say that an idea grows, even that it grows from the germ of a thought into a full-bodied concept! But although we speak of younger and older stages of the earth, we do not tend to speak of the earth as growing. If we say that nations grow, we hesitate to say that a civilization or a culture grows, although we do use other biological terms, such as the flowering of New England. Not just expansion, but expansion or increase that can with some justice be said to come from within that which expands, marks the edge of our application of the biological term "growth."

We also say of biological organisms that they are alive or living. Plants, animals, and men are the home-field of this term, but we also play with this term on other fields. We speak of groups of people for instance, a political party or movement, as alive or dead. In a quite different realm, we say an electric wire is alive when current is running through it, although we speak less than our ancestors did of a brook or stream being alive or having living water. We say an idea or a theory or a policy is alive, and we also speak of a live issue. But we do not ordinarily think of a government as being alive or dead. We say that a city is alive, but it seems odd to say that a country is alive, even if its people are on the whole lively, or more lively than some other folk. But can we say that some historical development such as industrialization or urbanization is alive? And surely it would not make sense to say that the world is alive, not to speak of the universe? The term works when we wish to indicate a certain activity or intensity or potential force, in contrast with an immediate and relatively inert background, so the difficulty of applying the term to the world or the universe is clear. With what would we be contrasting a living universe?

If this particular feature of language—the fact of there being edges to the areas within which our linguistic rules allow us to stretch the use of a word—is to help us understand the nature of religious discourse, however, we must above all examine the broad employment of words with which we speak of ourselves, not simply as living organisms but as persons. The language of belief is clearly related to how we speak of purposes and plans, of thinking, knowing, remembering, and loving, of being agents of our own actions and taking responsibility for our acts, and thus being conscious of ourselves. We may call this language about ourselves language about persons, or language about the self and other selves, or the language of mind. The home-field of such words is our own human life as linguistic beings. It is the most complex and richest area of our talk, and the one on which religion seems most to depend.

Talk about ourselves is first of all talk, and we have already seen some of the edges of the use of such words as "talking," "speaking," and even "language." When we speak of a talking parrot, we tend to put inverted commas around the word "talking," or to add that of course the parrot doesn't *really* talk. It repeats sounds it has learned to imitate, but *that* is not talking, even if it may be part of what we do in learning to talk. We also say, or some people do, that a picture speaks to them, although it seems out of place to ask what the picture says. History may or may not teach us something, but it does so without talking; the voice of history sounds suspiciously like the voice of the historian. And when "Russia says No," according to a newspaper headline, we are not surprised to find in the article which follows that in fact specific individuals did the talking.

Since we have already considered the limits of our talk about talk in the previous chapter, we could turn now to the self of which we speak. The workings of the word "self" in all its various combinations, however, are too complex for a short treatment. Think only of such diverse functions as emphasis ("Do it yourself!"), assuming responsibility ("I did it myself"), and specifying identity or essence ("I saw the marks it left, but not the animal itself"). This last example reminds us that the word "self" can also be used of animals and even objects, for we do speak of a self-lubricating bearing and a self-winding watch. Even the earth may be said to spin around itself, in both the senses of rotating on its axis, and also of doing this without a motor to keep it going. But what would it mean to say that the world is a self, that it is self-conscious, or dissatisfied with itself? Here too there are edges beyond which the word is not applied.

More useful for our investigation would be an examination of the edges of our language of mind, words such as "think." Human beings think, we say, on many different sorts of occasions. Consider only the following: "He thinks slowly," "He thinks before he speaks," "He thinks it will arrive tomorrow," "He thinks of his friend," "He thinks he is important." (If the old temptation to conceive of thinking as an inner process still pulls at us, it is because of a picture suggested by the first of this series of sentences, but surely not by the last.) The range of situations in which this word is used is evidently wide, but in each case we are speaking of a human being who, we say, is doing the thinking. The word is clearly to be applied to human beings.

Yet we do not apply the word to all human beings. I am not thinking here of a person of whom we should say that he never thinks. Although we could say, "Bill never thinks," we would not want to add that he does not know how. Whether in a particular case Bill actually thought would have to be decided on the evidence, but there is no problem about the application of the verb. The verb and its negation will work perfectly well. It is no breach of the rules of our language to say "Stop and think for once" to a friend of whom we have said that he never thinks. But should we say this to a baby? Does the baby wet his diapers because he has not stopped to think? Yet it seems not altogether right to say a baby simply cannot think, for we see the baby as growing into a being who can think. Before a child has learned the first rudiments of our language, however, it lives at or beyond the edge of the application of the verb "to think." Or, to put it better, we do not stretch the application of the verb so far as to cover the case of babies. The nearer the baby comes in growing up to doing the things that the rest of us do with language, the nearer he comes to the range within which the verb "think" can be used. So even before he has begun to talk, he may move from one place to another, push objects about, build a tower with blocks. As the behavior comes to resemble our own linguistic form of life, we come to feel more comfortable in using the language of mind here.

If it is clear that the helpless new-born infant lies outside the limits to which we can stretch the word "think," it is all the more clear that the word does not cover the case of the embryo. If someone were to say that several months before he was born he thought thus and so, we should not know what to reply.[5] What sense does this make? The difficulty with that remark is linguistic, not biological. Although we use the word "think" to cover a wide variety of situations, this one simply lies beyond the edge of language. The idea of a thinking foetus makes no sense at all, then, because it is not a part of our language. Which is to say, we can do nothing with it, except possibly take it as a joke.[6]

5. *P.I.*, §288.
6. We shall certainly return to this possibility at a later point, so let those with a sense of humor not feel that they are herewith being lightly dismissed.

The home-field for the verb "to think" is not simply the human being. It is the linguistically trained human being, the more or less mature adult, and the child as he comes to share the linguistic way of being in the world of adult human beings. As we run off the human chronological scale in the other direction, the same edge-characteristics appear. We have borderline cases, such as that, for example, of a person who has become almost totally paralyzed and been made speechless by a stroke. Movements of the eyes, perhaps, slight suggestions of a gesture or a change in facial expression give us some ground to say that he still thinks, but as these signs of participation in our usual linguistic world fade, we find it increasingly uncertain whether the verb can any longer be applied to him.

If there is doubt in the case just considered, there seems to be none once death arrives. A corpse does not think; that is a grammatical, not a physiological fact. The not unusual expression, "a dead person," already stretching the word "person" to its limit, marks the edge of our use of personal terms and the language of mind. Only in connection with some extended use of the word "life," as in the expression "life after death," should we be able to speak of those who have died as thinking, imagining, remembering, and the like.[7] Here again the model for this language is our use of these words in referring to living, speaking, human beings. It shows a decent if perhaps unconscious respect for the logic of our language that the biblical authors could only imagine a life after death as an embodied life.

Since human language and its associated behavior characterizes the home-field for the unambiguous use of the word "think," its application to animals becomes problematic. Animals do not talk, but when some of their behavior resembles ours (and this judgment will depend in part on our familiarity with the animals in question), we find we can stretch the word

7. This suggests that the difficulties some of us have with spiritualism are not so much scientific (doubts about the reliability of the evidence) as logical (doubts about "mental messages" coming from disembodied spirits).

to apply it to animals. It is within the rules of the use of this word to say that a dog thinks that someone is at the door. His attention is fastened on the door; he barks; he acts to some extent as one expecting someone to be there. But we do not say that he thinks someone will be at the door this time tomorrow.[8] Why not? Because we learn that a person thinks that someone will be coming tomorrow from his telling us so. We have no non-verbal way of letting each other know that we expect something in the future. Insofar as we use the word "think" of human beings on the basis of behavior other than speaking, to that extent we can say on the basis of similar animal behavior that an animal thinks, but in this instance we are approaching the edge beyond which the rules do not allow us to stretch the use of the word.

It would seem reasonable to suppose that we, who live further removed from animals than our ancestors, should find the range of application in this direction to be shrinking. People who live more closely to animals use the language of mind more freely with those animals, as is evident from the way in which animal-lovers speak. This shift in language usage is part of a shift in our form of life. On the other hand, we live more intimately with machines than did our ancestors, and this is reflected in our increasing agreement to stretch the language of mind to apply to some of these machines, which (we say) decide, remember, calculate, and think. We are still in the process of this transition, and therefore a consensus on these rules is still being formed. However, when a machine performs a task which if done by a human being would clearly involve thinking, we come increasingly to call it a case of thinking. As our form of life shifts further from contact with animals and toward closer association with machines, so the edges of our use of mind-words shift.

Although the edges of our application of the word "think" are in the process of shifting, no such shift seems to be evident in our terms for affections. A man may become fond of his car, may even pat it with affection, but we do not say that the

8. Cf. *P.I.*, p. 174.

car returns the affection, a claim which we frequently make for animals. A man may say his car is reliable and even that it is faithful, but hardly that it is affectionate or returns his love. This reflects the fact that our reliance on machines touches only certain aspects of our life.

Although our pattern of life is becoming less dependent on the forces of inanimate nature, we retain an ability to stretch some terms of personal activity in this area. We say that the sea roars, that a cloud is threatening, and that the sun smiles. Yet we have to admit that the sea roars, a cloud threatens, and the sun smiles mindlessly, if I may put it so. We do not say that the sea thinks, or that it roars because it has been offended. Clouds do not threaten in order to frighten us, nor to persuade us to act in a certain way, and the sun smiles without being pleased. The Newtonian model of a mechanistic universe, whatever its scientific liabilities, reflects or influences our way of speaking of the universe: being less inclined than men once were to speak of the world as having a soul, we speak of the world as running down, or turning at a certain rate. Here we come to the edge of our present patterns of applying such a word as "think." Other words, however, which also have their home-field in speaking of persons are (as we have seen) stretched even into this area of talk about the world. Not all but some of us would say that the earth suffers from what men are doing to it. Some would say that the earth is friendly to man, others that it is hostile. Some even say that the universe is friendly to man. In each case there is disagreement and uncertainty about the rules for such talk, which is to say that speaking differently of the earth, we live with this earth in different ways, for the agreements we have about language are agreements about our form of life.

We use other words to speak of ourselves, some of which we have mentioned in examining our stretchings of the word "think." Our use of such words as "remember," "love," or "decide" shows us that there too we begin with ourselves and stretch their application toward birth and death, running into the borderline cases of early childhood, progressing senility, or crippling disease. With animals we apply the terms in limited ways, coming soon to borders beyond which the words will not work because the rules have not been worked out for such cases. A dog may love his master, but do dogs love each other? The limit is shown by another of Wittgenstein's examples: "we say a dog is afraid his master will beat him; but not, he is afraid his master will beat him tomorrow."[9] Perhaps we shall agree to say that a machine can remember and decide as well as think, but shall we say that it can love or be in pain? With these other words, then, we find the same phenomena of border-line cases and limits beyond which we do not stretch the application of personal terms. Let us look at one more example, the verb "to intend."

People have intentions, intend things, have plans and purposes. As is generally the case in speaking of ourselves, what we say here is profoundly determined by the fact that we speak. If there are cases in which I can tell something of a man's intentions by the way he acts and the things he does, nevertheless there remains an ambiguity until he tells me what he intends. If I follow him and note that he buys a piece of pipe, dynamite, caps, electric wire, a battery, and a switch, I may well surmise that he plans to make a bomb or blow something up; but even if I witness the explosion, I will not know what he intended to blow up, or whether he succeeded in accomplishing the effect he intended. If I am able to guess correctly, I shall not know I was correct unless he tells me. The test for the proper use of the word "intend" lies in what people *say* they intend.[10] Such is our rule for the use of this word.

It is therefore difficult to stretch the application of "intend" and closely related terms to other realms. Does a hunting dog, when pointing, intend to indicate to us where the bird is?

9. *P.I.*, §650.
10. "It is in language that an expectation and its fulfillment make contact" (*P.I.*, §445). This conclusion (to the remarks beginning with §431, perhaps) will apply *mutatis mutandis*, I am arguing, also for an intention and its realization.

Ordinarily we just say that he points. Does the dog intend to find his way home? Again, should we not say simply that he finds his way home? On the other hand, we could say that a dog intended to fetch the stick we had thrown, but was distracted by the sudden appearance of a rabbit. It is fairly clear, however, that a machine does not intend to give us the answer or to do the task for which we employ it. There are border-line applications of the verb "to intend," and there is finally an edge to the area within which the term can be applied.

The related term "purpose," however, has been applied by some people to history. History has a purpose, some will say—even that the whole evolutionary process has a purpose. But this is closely related to saying that a machine has a purpose, namely, that for which it is employed, since those who say that history has a purpose presumably do not think of history intending its own purpose. The "purpose" is either the direction or course of events as they unfold, or that of someone who describes this direction, whether a man or a god. The terms "intention" and "purpose" have the roots of their use in the acting and speaking subject, man, and when the actor is not seen and will not or cannot tell us his intention or purpose, we have no rules to guide us in applying the words.

We shall carry no further these preliminary examinations of our use of certain words, trusting that we have said enough to bring out one feature of our language: the rules for our use of words permit us in most cases to stretch the application of these words into realms in which they may be less clear than on their home ground, until we come to areas in which they become either utterly ambiguous or totally unclear. At some point, an attempted application of the word loses touch with its rules.

We have seen, moreover, that the edges of applicability of any word or expression may change from time to time, as shifts occur in our way of living in the world. If we so choose, we can push out the edge of the use of any word, extending the range of its use and thereby expanding the rules for its application. *We* can, that is. Language as rule-governed behavior, as social convention, can expand or contract as this agreement is shifted, but we can carry through that movement only as an agreeing group, not as individuals. Since language is an agreement between men, the changes which take place can only be changes in this agreement. One cannot, alone, change *our* language.

Changes in language can of course be initiated by an individual. An individual can misuse language, break its rules, or extend the area of applicability of a word in such a way or under such circumstances that his new move is picked up by others. Others can come to share in what was a misuse to such a degree that this new extension is adopted as part of their language. So it is that a new word or a new use of a word may first be invented by one person, then be used by others, come to be included in a dictionary of slang, finally appear in a standard dictionary, and eventually come to be included only under the heading *archaic*, and even disappear from the standard dictionary entirely, only to come to rest in a dictionary of an ancient form of a language. When this movement takes place, what is occurring is a shift in what we have been calling the edges of language. In this way the edges of language can expand and contract.

There could never be, however, a case of going *beyond* the edges of language. An attempt to extend the application of a word, to apply it in a realm hitherto excluded by the rules of language, is an attempt to push out the edge. The speaker wants to do with language something slightly different from what has been done before. For example, he may want to bring out a connection, perhaps first of all for himself, between human thought and the activity of a machine, and so he says that the machine can think more clearly than he. That move, of course, has already taken place. But suppose that he were to say that a particular computer is in love with another computer. We should not be able to do anything with his remark, and unless he can in effect provide us with the conditions for its use, that is, with rules for this employment, he himself will not be able to do anything with his remark. He would have uttered nonsense, then, and could hardly be said to have gone anywhere, least of all beyond language. It would be less a case of *going* than of *ceasing* to use language altogether.

In speaking of computers being in love, he could have been proposing an extension of the rules for speaking of machines with terms used primarily of persons. And if we so chose, we could agree to use such an expression for the case of two computers which worked particularly well in tandem. If we lived closely enough with those machines, cared enough about their operation, became fascinated with what they could do and how they did it, we might want to make such an extension, applying to machines words hitherto reserved for persons and, within limits, to animals. Such a move would of course reveal much about us and our form of life. Indeed, I have had to specify what might be revealed in order to imagine the agreement which would underlie such an extension of the edges of this part of our language. I am not concerned with the merits of such a proposal, of course, but only with drawing attention to the existence of such edges, the possibilities of shifting any of these edges, and the way in which such shifts come about.

One can, if one prefers, have nothing to do with the edges of language. A man of limited imagination, no sense of humor, who likes to have everything clear, may prefer to stay well away from those areas in which words can be applied only at the cost of a certain ambiguity. Another man may exercise the full range of language right out to its edges. A third may try to push out those edges only at certain places. Those are the alternatives, with all degrees between them. But there is no going *beyond* the edges of language, for that would involve the contradiction in terms of saying what we cannot say. What we can say, our actual language, however, includes not only the relatively unambiguous home-field use of words, but also the edges of language, where we extend the application of words into other areas, and sometimes help to shift the edges of language. If this feature of our language is now a bit clearer, we may turn to consider what is actually going on when a man uses language at its edges.

CHAPTER VI
Speaking at the Edges of Language

Using language out near its limits is an unusual act. Not everyone may wish to behave in this way, and those who do speak at the edges of language from time to time have different ways of doing so and push, as we shall see, at different borders of our language. How and why anyone engages in such behavior is what we now wish to clarify by giving examples of pushing at the limits of language, remembering that to speak in a certain way is at the same time to live in a corresponding way.

We should say first, however, that it is not necessary to explore our linguistic frontiers at all. Indeed, reasons can be given for staying away from language's frontiers as consistently as possible. We saw that language tends to become ambiguous as it moves away from its clearly rule-governed center; it approaches nonsense at its limits, finally being so misused as not to be part of our language at all. But because language is so precious to us as our characteristic way of doing all that we do, its misuse is a threat to our humanity. To approach the point at which use turns to misuse, then, has its dangers.

More specifically, however, there are practical reasons for avoiding the edges of language, just as there are reasons for not skating out to where the ice is thin. Because we have so many practical things to do with language, which depend on our being clear and reasonably precise, it is often essential that there be as little ambiguity as possible in what we say. In designing and building airplanes or automobiles, for example, there is little room for ambiguity, certainly not if they are to be safe. In engineering, in scientific work, indeed in most of what we call practical affairs, getting the job done well depends on language doing its work clearly, and this is more likely to happen when words are used only within their home areas.

It is therefore characteristic of an acquisitive capitalist society such as ours to be suspicious of the borders of language. Skirting the fringes of nonsense is not the path of progress—as such a society measures progress. In a culture that wants business to be business, and no nonsense, fascination with the fringes of language will involve being at the fringes of society. The issue, seen in a linguistic perspective, is not whether the culture is too materialistic, whatever may be intended by that, but rather, which realms of language are to take cultural precedence. Economic forces in the West are undoubtedly pushing us to concentrate our manner of speaking—and living—in the more cut-and-dried areas where our words are unambiguous and the business of our society gets done. Thus value is measured in dollars, education becomes training for a career, and a work of art becomes an investment.

There may be, finally, more strictly personal reasons for preferring to ignore the edges of language. Some people just are more "down-to-earth," more practical-minded, more at home in the linguistic realm where things are unambiguous. Given a spectrum from order to disorder, clarity to puzzlement, there are always those who place themselves more on the side of order in their personal preferences and style of life. To such persons the edges of language will seem to comport too much of disorder, confusion, and the unknown. To speak and live in such an uncertain realm may call for more psychological security than many persons are able to muster. However we explain it, there is also this personal or perhaps psychological reason, as well as practical and cultural reasons, for staying away from the edges of language.

On the other hand, anyone fascinated by the edges of language will have other reasons to give in support of such linguistic behavior. He may be simply attracted by the unknown and by puzzles, and such an attraction can sometimes lead to discoveries, for discoveries are made, in John Wisdom's words, "not only by the scientists with microscopes, but also by the poets, the prophets, and the painters."[1] Those who explore the wilder regions of speech, Wisdom argues, can sometimes lead us to see the familiar in a fresh way, to discover things of which we had not previously been aware. Such discoveries, it could be argued, are one justification for frequenting the borders of language.

There is also what may be called a cultural reason for the choice to include the border areas of language as a working part of one's linguistic existence, since the choice reflects a judgment upon, and contributes to the shaping of, one's culture. The wider the spectrum of language a man employs, we argued in Chapter III, the richer is the world in which he finds himself. A decision to restrict language to unambiguous and clear realms, a decision to settle down near the center of our linguistic platform will be rejected by some people as too narrow an exercise of language. Such a narrowness results in a limited life in a limited world. The not uncommon complaint about our contemporary, technological, industrial culture (sometimes called secular culture) is that it is too flat, too unimaginative. If that judgment has any merit, we may wish to make room in our lives and in our society for the ambiguity, paradoxes, and puzzles of a wider, if wilder, use of language. To broaden our uses of language is to broaden the possibilities of life and of our apprehension of the world. Linguistic extravagance and irregularities are not accidental features of a "counter-culture."

The wish to frequent the edges of language can also be a personal reaction to what seems to be the stale orderliness of our society. The benefits of orderliness and regulation have

1. J. Wisdom, *Philosophy and Psychoanalysis* (Oxford: Blackwell, 1953), p. 154.

been so great, it could be said, that these become worshiped as ends in themselves, and that a healthy dose of disorder might then be necessary to make life human. Just how much confusion, just how large a dose of chaos, will be healthy is a matter of differing judgments about what it is to be human. Nevertheless, it can be argued that frontiers are in fact a feature of our language and our humanity, and that to exclude them is to place artificial and undesirable limits on our freedom. If such a line of thought reflects a personal preference, then there are personal as well as cultural reasons to be given also for moving out, at least from time to time, to the limits of language.

There is, however, more than one way of doing this. Since I shall argue that religion is one of these ways, it is fundamental for my argument first to describe examples of this behavior and show its variety. I shall therefore set religion aside temporarily and investigate some of the other ways in which people push at the limits of the application of words. By beginning with some of these other ways we may arrive at a position from which we can better assess the merits of thinking of religion as one case of this sort of linguistic behavior.

I said, in Chapter V, that attempts to overreach the rules for the application of words have no place in our language, except, possibly, as a joke. But now I want to develop this possibility and draw attention to the role which jokes—including puns—have in our language. It is an undeniable fact that making puns and jokes is part of our linguistic behavior. Indeed, one has only to imagine a language devoid of plays on words to realize that one would be imagining a form of life without humor, and therefore importantly different from the one we lead.

Puns, maligned as the lowest form of humor, are made by using one word or phrase in the place of a second which sounds the same but has a different meaning, or by employing a word which has two different uses in such a way as to recall both. So (as an example of the first) a door is not a door when

it is ajar. Or better, in reply to an old gentleman who for
reasons of health had recently had a small elevator installed in
his house and reported dreaming that it had taken him up, and
up, and right through the roof: "My!" was the reply, "that
must have made you soar!" One of Soupy Sales's more painful
lines will illustrate the second way of punning: "Show me a
lady shouting through a screen door and I'll show you a lady
straining her voice."

We play, however, not simply with similarities of sound and
differences of meaning, but (and this brings us back to our
subject) also with the limits to which we can stretch words.
An example would be the story of the comment of an official
and purely honorary pallbearer of the rich Texan who was
buried, according to the express instructions of his will, clad in
yellow silk pajamas, seated at the wheel of his salmon pink
Cadillac convertible. The grave having been dug out by a
bulldozer, the car placed in the hole, and the deceased having
been properly settled in place, the pallbearer, looking on,
remarked to a compeer, "Man, that's really living!" If one
finds this humorous, in a grim sort of way, it is because one is
struck by the fact that the pallbearer has stretched the word
"living" to cover a pathetic attempt to present death as one
more step in life—which is, to say the least, straining language
to the breaking-point.

Another example would be the conversation, if it may be
called that, between the White King and his Messenger, in
Lewis Carroll's *Through the Looking-Glass*, in which the
Messenger's huffy remark, that nobody walks faster than he
is contradicted by the King, for the reason that Nobody had
failed to outdistance the Messenger, so evidently Nobody was
the slower walker. Thus the word "nobody" is stretched
to the point of being used as a proper name, which violates
the rules for its use; and that is (if you are so inclined) a joke.

In the same book, Humpty Dumpty pushed the limits to the
limit, if it may be so put, by asking who is to be master, the
words or the user of words. When his remark, "There's glory
for you" is translated for commonsensical Alice as "There's a

SPEAKING AT THE EDGES OF LANGUAGE 103

nice knock-down argument for you," we reach the point at which language ceases to become a social convention and therewith ceases to be language. Lewis Carroll was evidently fascinated with the edges of language and his works are full of the results of his working just inside its limits. Humpty Dumpty, by asking who is to be master, is denying those limits and thereby in danger of becoming a character in search of an author!

The line between humor and nonsense is fine and not easily drawn. To any joke from Shaggy Dog stories to a fine play on words it can always be said, "But we don't say that!" And this is true, but it is also just the point. Wittgenstein remarked that grammatical jokes, depending as they do on the non-serious use of something as important as our language, "have the character of depth."[2] If the word "depth" is appropriate for situations in which we are left with something to think about, then it is appropriate to at least some humor. To play on words is to play with the tools of our human trade, with the basis of our whole intercourse with the world. It treats lightly what is, in most circumstances, of the utmost seriousness. And why not? Is there any reason why we should always be serious about ourselves or the world? If we were never serious, that would be another thing, but if we had not also this light-hearted use of words, this pattern of playing with language, then we should live less playfully in the world and therefore the world would be grimmer. For we often say that the person with a sense of humor sees the amusing side of life, and that the humorless person misses it. In making puns and jokes, a man behaves in a way that is different from that of the humorless man. He is teetering near the outer edge of our linguistic existence.

Explaining what is amusing is not itself amusing, however, so let us turn to another and more serious "misuse," or border-line use, of language, as we find it in the speech of lovers. Persons in love use words wildly or loosely. They say such things as "I love you more than all the world," "The stars in

2. *P.I.*, §111.

heaven cannot be compared to you." To call this exaggeration is too weak and misses the point. The language of love frequently touches the limits of our rules for the application of words. It moves along the furthest reaches of our ways of speaking of human feelings. Being in love is a case of teetering on the edge, sometimes even falling off the edge, of our linguistic platform. Indeed, lovers confirm this explicitly: "Words cannot express how much I love you," "Words cannot contain my love," "No words can possibly do justice to my love." The lover is impelled to the very limit allowed by our rules for the use of words. He thereby risks falling off into nonsense.

As I argued earlier, we misunderstand our language and therefore ourselves if we conclude from the speech of lovers that any experience, and specifically the experience of deep love, extends further than language, although the expressions just cited might tempt us to think so. If love really did extend beyond our language (whatever that would mean), it would be speechless. In fact, love is *not quite* speechless. Here too we must say that language goes as far as human life and experience do, even when it goes haltingly and stumbles. Language employed along its edges *is* halting, but it does just what is appropriate. That love is not for us an unambiguous matter of perfect simplicity and clarity, that it is of another sort than buying a pound of nails, is evident from the different linguistic behavior which it entails. "Words cannot do justice" is out of place for the pound of nails, but it does just what we want when we are speaking to our beloved. Here we find ourselves standing at what we have called, figuratively, the edge of our linguistic platform, and that calls for a tight-rope walker's linguistic balance and contortions, not the steady plodding appropriate to the center of that platform. Sauntering along with hands in pockets is all very well near the center of language, but when we find ourselves at our human limits, testing them to see if they will yield a bit, when we long out of devotion to another to push out into the unknown, then we find ourselves behaving rather differently. The linguistic aspect of that behavior, in this case, is the delicate balance: the falling and catching himself of the lover. Lovers can understand each other, nevertheless, since they go out to, not beyond, the edges of our linguistic experience.

There is a third way of playing with words, which only a few of us can handle but more can at least appreciate, and that is poetry. The poet, too, plays with words and stretches the possibilities to find new uses, new combinations of words. T. S. Eliot called poetry "a raid on the inarticulate."[3] By considering poetry as a form of walking the edges of language, along with humor and love, we are reminded, on the one hand, that delight in poetry is sometimes akin to delight in humor, and on the other, that some of the finest linguistic tributes to love have been made by poets.

The connections between poetry, humor, and love come out nicely in Auden's notes for a poem he never wrote, as he called them, in which the poet promises to love his beloved "even though all the stones of Baalbek split into exact quarters, the rooks of Repton utter dire prophecies in Greek, . . . and Paris and Vienna thrice be lit again by gas . . . ," yet hesitates to say, "I will love you whatever happens, even though you put on twenty pounds or become afflicted with a moustache"! His poem, Auden concludes, was to have expressed exactly what he meant when he thinks the words *I love you*, "but I cannot exactly know what I mean." Consequently, the poem remains unwritten.[4]

Twenty pounds or a moustache—there we have the realm of exactness. The wild language of poetry is amusing when it

3. T. S. Eliot, *Four Quartets*, "East Coker, V." Cf. *ibid.*, "Burnt Norton, V" (London: Faber & Faber; New York: Harcourt Brace Jovanovick, Inc., 1942, 1943):

> . . . Words strain,
> Crack and sometimes break, under the burden
> Under the tension, slip slide, perish,
> Decay with imprecision, will not stay in place,
> Will not stay still . . .

4. W. H. Auden, *Homage to Clio* (London: Faber & Faber, 1958; New York: Random House, Inc., 1960), pp. 50-51.

is contrasted with such mundane images. Humor and love show up as near neighbors to poetry, for all three play close to the realm of nonsense. Therein lie their power, charm, and fascination.

This gives us another way to see why poetry cannot be translated into prose. To attempt it is to move away from the edges of language and back into the clarity of language's central plains, and that very move takes us away from where the poet was standing. We shall no longer feel his difficulties, nor see his discoveries, nor share his vision if we will not move with him out to the farthest edges of language. It is the experience of standing there that the poet opens for us, and to "translate" his words into clearly definable terms is to destroy the essence of his art. If we need to ask what a poem means, expecting an answer appropriate to the unambiguous realms of language, we show that we completely misunderstand what poetry is. The poet, like the lover and the humorist, says just exactly what he wants to say; his inexactitude suits precisely the needs of his raid on the inarticulate. Poetry is linguistic behavior appropriate to experiences of perceptions that lead us to stretch words. To ask the poet to try again without stretching his words is to ask him to cease being a poet.

The edges of language are also reached, from time to time, in the work of metaphysics. This is a difficult matter to deal with, however, not only because metaphysicians disagree in their results, but because they disagree even about the definition of their field. One man's metaphysics is another man's logic. This branch of philosophy has also undergone considerable change over the past half century, and what I am calling metaphysics, some would assign to other branches of philosophy. I am not concerned to take a stand on philosophical nomenclature, however. If others prefer to read "philosophy" whenever I have written "metaphysics," I should have no objections, for this has no bearing on the point I want to make.

Without hoping to meet every philosopher's requirements, then, we shall define metaphysics as the attempt to clarify the foundations of our thought and the fundamentals of our language. By sorting out and clarifying the kinds of things that we say, we can be led to see more clearly what we have been looking at all along but have not sufficiently noticed. However loose this definition may be, it will do for our purposes, for it allows us to come to the questions which most would accept as metaphysical, such as whether it is possible to know what we claim to know, whether we can really know other minds, and even whether metaphysics itself can tell us anything about the world.[5] When we are plagued by such questions, which put in doubt our commonest assumptions, we can feel ourselves coming close to madness! As one metaphysician has said, "In the labyrinth of metaphysics are the same whispers as one hears when climbing Kafka's staircases to the tribunal which is always one floor further up."[6] Questions which probe our seemingly innocent and otherwise unquestioned uses of such basic words as "know," "see," "world," "cause," and "fact" force us to tread the limits of our thought because they take us to the edges of our use of these words.

Consider some of the problems which are generally considered to fall within this realm. William James called "the most pregnant issue in philosophy" the question whether the world is one or many. As he saw it, it is one in a number of different ways, depending on the frame of reference. It is one world for the physical sciences, and one world for economics. It is one world for communications and transportation, and one world for political analysis. By the same token, however, it is also many, since it is one world in each of these ways. If it is asked, however, "But is it ultimately one or ultimately many; is there some final, deeper unity behind all the plurality

5. Such in any case are some of the questions which John Wisdom, for many years professor of metaphysics at Cambridge, regarded as metaphysical questions. Cf. especially his "The Metamorphosis of Metaphysics," republished in his *Paradox and Discovery* (Oxford: Blackwell, 1965), chap. 6.
6. J. Wisdom, *Philosophy and Psychoanalysis*, p. 282.

of unities which can be detected?" then we find with James
that we are almost at a loss to say. Almost—for in fact James
dared to risk an answer.[7] Our concern is not with James's or
any other answer, however, but rather, with a peculiar feature
of the question and the consequent strains placed upon any
answer. The contrast of unity and plurality is clear enough
when we examine a small piece of our universe: Does that
box contain one apple or many? The contrast between the two
is fairly unambiguous when applied to a subject of limited
scope. But the question of a final unity pushes the distinction
to ever wider reaches, and finally (is this really only one step
further, or does it not change the nature of the question?) it attempts to apply it to the whole of our experienced universe. Will
the distinction between one and many bear such stretching?
Where is the limit beyond which the rules for its working no
longer guide us? The sense of giddiness that comes at this point
is a sign that we are stumbling along one edge of our language.

There are other frontiers. Can we ever really know what is
in another man's mind? Can we even know that there are
other minds? Of course in our ordinary affairs we certainly
assume that we can; we act as if we did. But can we really
know, or is our knowing only a well-established habit of
guessing? Here, as so often in metaphysical questions, we find
the telltale word "really," which plays somewhat the same role
as the word "ultimately." What is being asked is not whether
we can know at all, but whether we can *really* know, know
absolutely surely, know with the certainty of God (we may
say) what is in another's mind. But does this extended use of
"know" fall within the range of ways we generally agree to
use it? The word "know" is being pushed to its limits, demands
of perfection being placed upon our knowledge of other minds
that are hardly appropriate to the case.

Some would say that the question about the meaning of life
is also a metaphysical question. Note that what is wanted is

7. Cf. my "William James and Metaphysical Risk," in *Theological
Explorations* (New York: The Macmillan Company, 1968; London:
S.C.M. Press, 1968).

not *a* but *the* meaning of life. Once more the question is itself puzzling because it pushes the word "meaning" near to—some would say, over—the edge of its agreed use. We ask about the meaning of this or that event: a window that was closed is found open upon our returning to the house we had left locked, which probably means that we have been robbed; or a political figure is dismissed from his position, which may mean that he has committed some indiscretion, but it may also mean that a conflict within the government has come to a head and been resolved in favor of those who remain in office. Single events are said to have meaning when we can gather something from them, draw some conclusion about their context.[8] But asking about the meaning of life is like asking about the meaning of the world, and even like asking about the cause of the universe. Will the word work way out there or has this use not dropped off the edge, such that it is not clear whether the question makes sense?

The frontier of language to which the metaphysician is driven is signaled sometimes by the words "ultimately" and "really" (as we have noted), but also sometimes by the use of paradox. To say that the world is ultimately not one but many, or that we never really know other minds, or that there cannot be a meaning to life, seems on the face of it to be false, or at least in need of being balanced by its contrary statement.[9] For there is some unity to the world, and we know something of other minds, and life has some meaning. The paradoxical things which metaphysicians say, however, can bring us to see an aspect of the matter which we may not have seen so well before, or had seen but not noted. And by bringing us to see aspects of others or the world in a fresh way, we come also to see new aspects of ourselves. By pushing at the edges of our language and so of our thought with such questions, we incur the possibility of nonsense or the danger of madness, but there is also the opportunity for discovery. That is the reward of risking ourselves on the borders of our language.

8. Cf. *P.I.*, §543.
9. Cf. J. Wisdom, *Philosophy and Psychoanalysis*, pp. 262f.

Without claiming to have exhausted the field, we shall mention one other form of speaking at the edges of language (which we shall consider in greater detail later), and that is religion. Religion too is linguistic behavior. I have admitted that it is other things as well, but if we recall what I have said about the way in which our language is embedded in, and interwoven into, our whole human existence, then, as I have argued, it is not a mistake to regard religion as linguistic behavior. It takes many different forms, of course: prayer, preaching, theology, corporate cultic activities, singing, and conversations. In each of these, most of the time, language will be working well within its borders. A man might ask the person next to him to pass him that book of prayers, for example, or say to another that he found some theologian's book most helpful, or ask his wife if she brought any money for the collection. These cases involve a well-regulated, unambiguous use of words, far from the edges of nonsense.

These examples, however, would hardly be considered to have anything to do with religion at all, if there were not a quite different aspect to religion which gives it its distinctive character. What marks linguistic behavior as religious is the fact that it is another form of walking the edges of language, marked by speaking in paradoxes, stammering, and also silence. Religious people say such things as "God is personal, but not a person, almighty and loving, yet he allows evil to happen." This and other paradoxical assertions must leave us wondering whether language can be pushed that far out from its rule-governed center. Religious people use metaphors, parables, and other indirect ways of making their point. They speak of the impossibility of knowing the God in whom they say they believe, they point to the smile of the Buddha as the only answer to men's questions, or they try to stop them with the *koans* of Zen. They say that reason is not acquainted with the reasons of the heart, or that the greatest wisdom of man can be only silence. Even fairly ordinary believers will admit that their belief is close to nonsense, and it is evident that they are as aware as others that their words often break down.

The words the believer uses in speaking of the "object" of his belief are at best ambiguous, since he feels driven to extend them to the limit of the area within which their rules work. He too is aware that what he says barely makes sense. Because he wants to say as much as could possibly be said, the believer balances on the edges of language and therefore risks a fall into nonsense.

Consider some cases. St. Paul, presumably a master of prayer, insisted that he did not know what to say when he prayed, "but the Spirit himself intercedes for us with signs too deep for words" (Romans 8:26). Whatever commentators and theologians may try to make out of that, it is clear enough that St. Paul had gone right to the limit of language. Again, in discussing the resurrection, he said that there are different sorts of flesh, as that of men, animals, birds, and fish (which is already stretching things a bit), and there are different sorts of bodies, those on the earth, and those in the sky, but then he goes to the breaking point in saying that there is a physical body and a spiritual body (1 Corinthians 15:39–44). Theologians may wish to say much about the difference between this distinction of the physical and the spiritual and a distinction of the material and the immaterial. What is evident in any case is that the word "body" has been stretched to its breaking-point, to the point beyond which its use would no longer be rule-governed, and so no longer a part of our language. This pressing of words to their limits is central to the linguistic behavior which is religion.

A similar stretching of language characterizes modern religion also. A case in point is Martin Buber's well-known extension of the word "thou," which has its home-field, as he points out, in one human being addressing another. Without assessing what Buber considers to be going on in the process, it is clear that he thinks this word can at times be addressed even to a tree, and finally to the whole world. To address the universe as "thou" is surely to stretch the application of the pronoun to a point at which it must be wondered what has happened to the rules for its use. Yet this is surely the religious use of the term in Buber's writings. Once more religion shows up linguistically as a case of speaking at language's edges.

Religion, then, is one more way, though not the only way, of moving along the edges of language, pushing words to the limit of the conventions for their usage. We shall see in due course that religion has its peculiar way of doing this, but at this stage of the argument I want only to argue that religion, along with humor, poetry, and aspects of metaphysics, is marked by this linguistic feature. These are some of the ways in which men balance on the edges of linguistic conventions, at the very limits of our language.

Plays on words, the wild loose talk of lovers, metaphysical paradoxes, and the contradictions and extravagances of religion are all attempts to go as far as possible with words, to say the very most that our language permits. A desire, a longing to push out the limits of some particular area of our language, implies that there is a realm of discourse and life in which our ordinary, or rule-governed, behavior does not seem to be adequate. The speaker may feel more strongly than most about the area in question, he may see aspects of it that others have not noticed, or he may have come to see this area in what is at least for him a new way, one for which familiar ways of speaking no longer serve. For whatever reason, he now wants to say something which requires stretching the rules of language.

The areas of life and language in which this longing arises can vary. The poet's longing may arise in any area. The lover will be passionately concerned for his beloved. The Christian, as we shall see later, longs to say all he can about himself and others as persons with a past and a future. In each case, the sort of behavior which we are considering is occasioned by a longing to extend the limits of what our language allows, to say more than the established conventions of language permit, regardless of the area of life and language in which this may arise. Instead of saying, "I want to say the very most that could conceivably be said," he says something not at all straightforward, something paradoxical perhaps, something close to the nonsensical.

If by "rational" we mean that which lies within the clear and unambiguous realms of language, then it is analytically true that speaking at the edges of language is not rational. The speaker wants contrary ends at once: he wants both to use language and to extend (and thereby break) the conventions that make language the social institution that it is. His longing leads him necessarily to risk falling into nonsense.

This analysis simply corroborates what has often been said of humorists, lovers, metaphysicians, and religious persons, who have often been called fools. The merits and demerits of their linguistic behavior and the longing that leads to it have already been considered and there is no need to say more here. Whether we choose to call this longing and this behavior unreasonable or irrational depends on how each of us weighs those merits. As we have said, not everyone will share the concerns or feel the longings which can lead a person to linger at the edges of language, but there are humorists, lovers, poets, metaphysicians, and religious persons who do, in their several ways—at least from time to time.

The human activities which we have considered as various forms of walking the edges of language are sometimes confused with each other. People have found poets, lovers, and metaphysicians funny. Sometimes people have said that metaphysics is only poetry, or that religion is really metaphysics, and vice versa, or that some poetry is either metaphysics or religion. If we are at all right in seeing a common linguistic feature in these activities, the confusion becomes more understandable and tolerable. Although it is a confusion, it points up the fact that these activities have a common feature: in each one of them language is from time to time stretched out to the breaking-point. Each arises in part from a longing to go to the limits of what we are able to say. If this extended use is measured by that of the clearest, least ambiguous use of words, it will seem at least unclear, probably ambiguous, and at most nonsense. Nevertheless, stretching words is part of the linguistic behavior of mankind. The examination of this practice can lead us closer to understanding religion, which is itself one form of speaking at the edges of language.

CHAPTER VII
The Linguistic Frontiers of Christianity

Speaking at the edges of language and straining its limits from time to time is a necessary, although not a sufficient, condition for religion in general and therefore for Christianity in particular. It is necessary, for without this there would be no religion, as we shall show. This feature is not a sufficient criterion of religion, however, for we have admitted that there are other ways of walking the edges of language than religious ways. The feature which distinguishes religion from these other linguistic activities will occupy us in the next chapter; in this chapter I want to concentrate on religion alone and to identify the particular segment of language which is of particular concern to Christians. Christianity does not push just generally against the limits of language; it pushes at a particular point, or along a particular section.

The fact that religion consists linguistically in pushing at certain edges of language is the result of a longing, an intensity of concern, a passion for some aspect of our linguistic existence. It is conceivable that one could long to say the utmost that could be said on any topic. The beauty of nature or its cruelty, for example, might move a person to linguistic extravagance approaching nonsense. A sense of the order of nature or human life could stimulate a similar response. Recalling our image of a platform, we can think of the edges of language as lying along the circumference of our rule-governed linguistic behavior, and there is no reason in principle why we might not long to push that circumference outward at any point, to begin from any part of our linguistic activity and strain at its limits.

A religion could reasonably be expected to manifest a particular pattern as men pushed out toward one specific edge of our language. As an example, one might think of a religion which took its point of departure from speaking of the balance of nature. It could be said that nature exhibits a pattern of interacting opposites. There are male and female, day and night, winter and summer, land and sea. This is simply how things are, it might be thought, and some people might leave it at that. Others might become so fascinated by this pattern, however, that they would want to do more than "leave it at that." They might speak of the way of nature, of the balance and harmony by which the rain falls on the mountains, runs down to the sea to arise and fall again as rain, slowly wearing the mountains down and bringing land and sea to a single level. They might then say that this pattern is not just based on how we look at nature, on distinctions which we choose to draw, but that it is an expression of the final truth about all things. These people might push farther and say that this way of nature expresses a further Way, so much more basic to the world than anything which we can describe that it surpasses our understanding. They might finally come to say, with the Taoist, that "the way that can be spoken is not the real Way."[1] The limit of speaking of balance and harmony has been reached and beyond this can lie only silence. That is the particular edge of language on which the Taosit religion teeters.

According to William James, religion "consists of the belief that there is an unseen order, and that our supreme good lies in harmoniously adjusting ourselves thereto."[2] Apart from the

1. The opening warning of the *Tao Teh Ching*. On the variety of possible translations, see Philip Wheelwright, *Metaphor and Reality* (Bloomington: Indiana University Press, 1968), p. 175.
2. William James, *The Varieties of Religious Experience* (London: Longmans Green & Co., 1902), p. 53.

dubious notion that religion consists in a belief (we have already expressed our reservation on that point in Chapter II), this definition suffers from the use of a word—"unseen"—which misses the peculiar linguistic pattern of religion: we should better say "unspeakable" instead. If religious persons believe in, or, as we should prefer to say, persist in speaking of, a Way (or order), then we should note that they speak of it as beyond the adequacy of their words. They are convinced that the *Tao* that can be spoken is not the real *Tao*. Most religions manifest the behavior of those who have run into the limits of some area of language, although not necessarily those of the Taoist. The best that can be done, it seems to the religious person, is to fluctuate between silence and the indistinct borders of language.

This example provides an important clue to the similarity of religions as well as to their differences. Religions are similar in that they share the feature of language stretched to its limits. In the profoundest expressions of the belief, faith, or way of life of any religious tradition, the borders of language are pushed out to the point of paradox, near nonsense, and silence. But where this pushing occurs reveals the differences between religions, for they differ in the particular sectors of language from which they depart, and the particular segments of the circumference of language at which they push. One religion may tread the edges of our talk about the balance of nature, another those of talk about the self, a third the borders of speaking of a piece of human history, and yet another may push to the limits of our talk about law or order. The varieties of religious possibilities are as wide as our language.

This way of considering the matter accounts for the fact that deeply religious persons of different traditions seem often to have a mutual sympathy, to be "on the same wave-length," so to speak, and yet to disagree—sometimes radically—on the "message." It might be said that they "speak the same language," for they share a common linguistic behavior pattern. They are both inhabitants of the border regions of our language and they recognize each other as such. In another sense, however, they do not "speak the same language," since they inhabit different, and sometimes radically different, linguistic frontiers.

In order to make clear the logic of the particular religious position under investigation, then, we must identify which borders of language are occupied or visited from time to time by a contemporary, educated, Western Christian. A century ago, Matthew Arnold, who was concerned in his own way with the logic of a contemporary form of biblical religion, proposed morality as the area of life which preoccupied the biblical authors so that they strained its language to its limits. He was convinced that this area and its language could hold the same fascination for Christians in his time. He did not, of course, define the matter in the terms I have just used, yet the parallel is close enough to warrant attention, even if his idea that moral language was the heart of biblical religion seems inadequate.

As Arnold saw it, biblical religion centered in one overriding concern, one object which mattered supremely, and that was conduct, which comprises "three-fourths . . . at the very lowest computation, of human life," including "eating, drinking, ease, pleasure, money, the intercourse of the sexes, the giving free swing to one's temper and instincts." "These are the matters," he argued, "with which conduct is concerned, and with which all mankind knows and feels it to be concerned."[3] Right conduct is religion's concern, and the biblical term for this, as Arnold pointed out, is "righteousness." Indeed, he thought this was the object of all religion.

However, morality and religion are not identical. The difference between them, Arnold said, is a matter of degree. "Religion, if we follow the intention of human thought and human language in the use of the word, is ethics heightened, enkindled, lit up by feeling; the passage from morality to religion is made when to morality is applied emotion. And the

3. Matthew Arnold, *Literature and Dogma* (1873). References are to the edition published in *Dissent and Dogma* (Ann Arbor: University of Michigan Press, 1968), pp. 172f.

true meaning of religion is thus, not simply *morality*, but *morality touched by emotion*."[4] To the question how this application comes about, Arnold's answer was: "Why, how does one get to feel much about any matter whatever? By dwelling upon it, by staying our thoughts upon it, by having it perpetually in our mind."[5] And just this was what made the people of Israel distinctive: "No people ever felt so strongly . . . that conduct is three-fourths of our life and its largest concern. No people ever felt so strongly that succeeding, going right, hitting the mark in this great concern, was the *way of peace*, the highest possible satisfaction."[6] Thus Arnold defined biblical religion in part by locating its concern in conduct or morality, and in part by insisting upon the depth of concern, the intensity of longing, the extent to which this concern is pushed.

Moreover, attentiveness to right conduct led Israel to what Arnold regarded as a special feature of morality: "the very great part in righteousness which belongs, we may say, to *not oneself*."[7] With this expression Arnold meant to indicate aspects of righteousness that are not of our own making, nor within our power: that three-fourths of our life is conduct, that doing right is satisfying, and that our conduct and degree of doing right is not wholly under our control. In short, an important part of what may be said about our conduct does not concern our own activity. This "not ourselves" is what Israel adored and loved under the name 'Yahweh.'[8]

This argument, however, is not without its problems. Defining the "not ourselves" as he did, Arnold in effect made it equivalent to certain very general anthropological facts. Thus there is the danger that the "not ourselves" becomes, after all, ourselves, although ourselves other than as moral beings. Ourselves as biological and social beings of a certain sort (concerned with conduct, not fully controlling our conduct, satisfied when conduct is right) would then account for all that could be said about our conduct in other than moral terms.

4. *Ibid.*, p. 176   5. *Ibid.*, pp. 178f.   6. *Ibid.*, p. 180.
7. *Ibid.*, p. 181.   8. *Ibid.*, pp. 181–83.

This is hardly what Arnold wanted to maintain, for he began
his analysis by drawing a sharp distinction between two uses
of language, the scientific and the literary. The terms of
science are used for exact knowledge and for "perfectly definite
and ascertainable" ideas, whereas literary terms are, in his
words "thrown out, so to speak, at a not fully grasped object
of the speaker's consciousness."[9] Since the whole point of
Arnold's argument was to show that 'Yahweh,' or 'God,' is a
literary term, 'God' could not be equivalent to a "not ourselves" of which we can have definite and ascertainable knowledge, namely, man's biological and social character. 'God'
thus turns out to be both a literary and a scientific term, which,
by definition, is impossible.

Arnold's distinction between the two sorts of terms or language is too sharp and too exclusive; we use language in more
ways than can be dreamt of in his philosophy. We could, however, go back to the point where his difficulty arises and ask
about the adequacy of his interpretation of what is going on
when we dwell on, or have "perpetually in our mind," some
matter of great moment, such as right conduct. I would suggest that what is going on is that we have come to the limit of
applicability of our words, where we speak paradoxically, or
contradictorily. We may then say indeed that the most important part of what we do is not of our doing. We might even
speak of a "not ourselves that makes for righteousness." We
should have arrived at the point which I have been calling
the edge of language, the edge, specifically, of moral language.

If to speak of a "not ourselves that makes for righteousness"
is speaking at the borders of language, however, then the logic
of this expression cannot be that of the well-regulated language of moral argument or exhortation. Its logic is that of the
frontiers of such language, which means that it lies just at the
limit of what can be said, approaching nonsense or falling off
into silence. The use of this expression is one way of behaving
when we long to say the most that could possibly be said

9. *Ibid.*, p. 171.

about righteous conduct because it matters to us so much, and we feel that our words are inadequate. That too, if you will, is a fact about ourselves, but it is a fact about our linguistic existence. On this interpretation of Arnold's thesis, the "not ourselves" is not a reference to some very general facts of human nature; it is an example of a specific aspect of human life in this world. It is one case of linguistic behavior appropriate to standing at the edges of language. To say "not ourselves," then, is another way of saying that we want to say the very most that could be said on this subject, but are not sure what that would be.

The question remains, however, whether Arnold found the correct subject matter of biblical religion. Is conduct, as he so broadly defined it, the special object of the biblical authors? And did he distinguish Christianity from Judaism accurately when he said, "The Old Testament says: *Attend to conduct!* the New Testament says: *Attend to the feelings and dispositions whence conduct proceeds!*"?[10] It was common in the nineteenth century to regard Christianity and the New Testament as internalizations of Judaism and the Old Testament. The liberal spirit of many theologians of the nineteenth century (and not only of that period) had difficulty with the public or external character of Israel's religion. This is only another example of the perennial difficulty which Christians have had in acknowledging the central role of Law in the Old Testament. Earlier we argued that religion has a public character because it is a linguistic activity. The Old Testament made this point in another way: it placed Law in so important a position that religion could not become an inner matter. Even if Jeremiah could imagine a better future in which religion would be from the heart, he nevertheless imagined it as having a *law* written in the heart! The role of Law in the Old Testament stands as Israel's perennial warning: "try not to think of religion as an inner process at all!" Insofar as Christianity remains committed to reading the Old Testament as well as the New, it is committed to listening again and again to that

10. *Ibid.*, p. 221.

warning. Arnold has not been alone in failing to heed that
warning.

Apart from reservations about interpreting New Testament
religion as an internalized version of that of the Old Testament, we would still question whether conduct was the central
object of concern for biblical religion. If the biblical writings
consisted only in laws, it would be difficult to quarrel with
Arnold's interpretation, but in fact, the Bible contains more
than law. Moreover, the manner in which laws are introduced
in the Old Testament points in a direction slightly different
from the one in which Arnold looked. Israel's concern was not
simply with conduct, but with the *story* of conduct, not just
with Law, but with the history of a Law received, disobeyed,
and given again. The Israelites were haunted not by their own
conduct, but by the story they told of their conduct, the story
of one event following upon another, in a word, with *history*.
This was the area of language whose edges they pushed. They
told the story of their own past, they projected that story into
a fantastic future, they told it dramatically and poetically, to
the outer limits of understandable language.

Following this interpretation, apocalypticism appears as an
essential part of Israel's literature, not an unfortunate excre-
scence. Christians who are embarrassed by apocalyptic writing
and try to hide it under the milder category "eschatological"
misunderstand the logic of their religion. If talk of the past
leading on into talk of the future moves from clear, unambiguous rule-governed behavior into behavior appropriate to
language's borders, an apocalyptic way of speaking is surely
to be expected. Israel's interest in history included fairly
"objective," unambiguous reporting, of which the record of
King David's difficulties with his son Absalom is an example,
but if one became obsessed with Israel's whole story and
believed oneself to be a part of it, if one felt that reports of
"the facts" were but a fraction of what needed to be said, then
one might well paint images as dramatic and fantastic as those
found in biblical apocalypticism. The apocalyptic writings of
the Bible are language about the history of righteousness—

and unrighteousness!—gone wild, right up to and nearly over the edge of that very language.

Does Christianity push at the edges of this same area of discourse? Well, it depends upon *which* Christianity one has in mind, for as we have seen, Christianity has come in many different forms. There has surely been the Christianity of personal feeling and the inner life, manifested in pietisms of many periods. But another important strain of Christianity has shared with biblical religion a fundamental concern for history, and this concern is not uncommon among contemporary educated Christians in the West. It is in order, therefore, to examine commitment to history as the chief area of discourse at whose edges Christians push.

The conventions of ordinary discourse of the first century and of the twentieth century are of course not necessarily the same. When we suspect or can identify a difference, we shall indicate which period we are discussing. The fact that we can read and understand first-century authors, however, and can even grasp fairly well some of the distinctions they made between, for example, the ordinary course of events and extraordinary happenings, shows that the rules have not changed radically. They as well as we could distinguish straightforward reports about an emperor from the extended use of language developed for the imperial cult. Unless otherwise noted, therefore, we shall assume a basic continuity in the rules for the use of words.

For almost any variation of Christianity, the central and controlling figure has been the man Jesus of Nazareth. The form of the four Gospels testifies to the interest of early Christians in the *story* of this man's life. And the history of Jesus of Nazareth has defined for Christians the other key terms they employ, such as "love," "faith," "hope," and 'God'. Love, for example, is defined in more than one piece of New Testament writing by what happened in the history of Jesus.

That history is told both in the unambiguous, clear terms, appropriate to the center of linguistic behavior, and in the loose, almost nonsensical use of language on its borders. His birth is dated by the common system of Roman usage, by giving the names of the emperor and the local governor; key moments in his life are connected with common occurrences and figures of unambiguous history, such as public feasts and ecclesiastical and political leaders; he was condemned to death for violation of Roman political policy and law. It is evident, however, that his followers wanted to say of him more than an ordinary, rule-governed report of the time and significance of events would allow. His coming is therefore spoken of as occurring "in the fullness of time" (Galatians 4: 4), hardly their usual system of dating. And, although almost any historical occurrence can be said to have consequences, this man's life and death were said to have *eternal* and *universal* consequences. Such statements push to the point of nonsense even first-century (not to speak of twentieth-century) ordinary ways of making historical judgments.

It can sometimes be said that a certain historical person was a good man. It was said of Jesus that he "went about doing good" (Acts 10: 38). But that was hardly the end of the matter for the New Testament authors. From there they pushed out to speaking of this man as not only perfect, not only sinless, but as the very righteousness of God (Romans 3: 21), an expression that stretches the limits of moral judgments almost to the breaking-point! A rule-governed, historical estimate would have said that Jesus was a good Jew, a faithful Jew. Instead, the New Testament makes the wild utterance that he was Israel itself, even a new Israel! His life was, of course, that of a man, but it was said in addition of him that he was a second Adam, a sort of man-written-all-over-again. This is what "faith" in Jesus amounted to, this more than extravagant language about him, which pushes the conventions for speaking of human history to such an extent that some would call this talk foolishness.

It has been said of men that some of their deeds live after them, while others are interred with their bones. It has been said of some men that they had great influence on the course of history or on the lives of others, that the world is different as a result of their life and work. Such things have sometimes been said in admiration and sometimes they have been spoken as sober judgments. But the early Christians said of Jesus that after his death he rose from the dead and was now the sovereign over history! They did not seem concerned to argue that some strange thing had happened to the cells of his dead body, but they clearly wanted to say that his history, far from stopping with death, began anew and with universal consequences. In the mouths of the earliest Christians and their followers, their and our ordinary talk about history and the influence of historical persons was stretched to the breaking-point, and a term was used that does not obtain in ordinary discussion of history even in the first century, and one that from the scientific historian's point of view can only be called nonsensical: resurrection. To say that a man's history in the world continues after his death, and that it will continue as long as there is any history of the world at all, is to stretch speaking of men's histories almost beyond recognition.

It may be said that some men are particularly close to their fellow men, that they share the joys and sorrows of others. The Christians, however, said of Jesus that, in some strange way, he *was* every other man, and that all mankind was therefore involved in his history. They said that his history is ours. The breech with our rules for speaking of men's lives is evident. It has been said that no man is an island unto himself, and that therefore any man's death diminishes each of us, that therefore we need not send to ask for whom the bell tolls, since it tolls for us. But the New Testament pushes further and says that "as in Adam all die, even so in Christ shall all be made alive" (I Corinthians 15:22). When the Christian speaks of what he can hope for in his own history, therefore, he speaks—of all things—of resurrection! Here again, as in speaking of Jesus, this is not an utterance concerning biology. It is a word which marks the breaking-point, the outer edge of historical judgment.

It is well known that Christianity leads men to speak of resurrection, and not of an immortal soul or spirit. The

Christian is up against the limits of speaking, not of some
aspect of himself such as the soul or spirit, but rather, of himself in his full involvement with others, a person with a concrete past. If the Christian looks to a future, it is a future for
that full historical person, including the social relationships
which are a large part of historical existence.

The focus of Christian discourse, then, the solid, rule-
governed area of speaking, out to whose edges it is stretched,
is the history of one man in the context of the history of a
people, Israel, who had already pushed language to its limits
in speaking of their own past and future. In stretching to the
edges of such talk, Christians spoke of that history as leading
on into their further history, and finally as the key to the
history of all mankind. To share in this linguistic behavior
was to be a Christian.

It should be noted that when I identify "history" as the
special subject of Christianity, I am using the term in a way
unacceptable to a historian. The historian deals only with
the past. However, although the Christian focus on "history"
looks back, it also looks ahead, and it sees past and future as
intimately related. It begins with the past, but it is more
deeply concerned with what is going to be. For the historian
this is too broad a vision to be called "history." The word has
already been stretched to cover a wider subject, since it is an
important aspect of the Christian's interest in the past that he
see the past as moving ahead to the future. Or to put the point
in less ambiguous terms, he sees his life and that of every
man as having both a past and a future, and it is the *whole*
as yet unfinished story that interests him.

The Christian community has been another topic of concern
that has led believers to stretch language. An important part of
the interest of Christians in human history has been turned to
their life in a community with others who also say that they
share in the further history of Jesus of Nazareth in this world.
This community consists of particular individuals living in
various circumstances and involved in various relationships.
This much can be said quite unambiguously. But Christians

have wanted to say more than this, more than is usual with rule-governed speech about human communities. Consequently they stretched their language for speaking of social groups and called their community the body of Christ, the garden of God, the bride of Christ, the saints—terms which make no historical or sociological sense. No wonder, for here too we are at the edges of language.

Finally, Christians spoke of an end, a final revealing of the meaning of all history, in which all mankind would see clearly that no man's history is finally lost or forgotten. Indeed, everything in the world would find its place in this new "order." Such language distorts any rules we have for speaking of that which might conceivably happen. So wild was some of this speaking, this outer limit of saying, "History counts! Every man's history counts!" that Christians themselves have sometimes been uneasy in its presence. And with the word "resurrection" we come to the very outer reaches of speaking of ourselves as persons with a story to tell, that is, a history, in which nothing is lost. So near is this to dropping off the edge, so imprecise is the border line between the farthest possible stretching of language and utter nonsense, that even Christians too have been uneasy with it. Yet to protest at this point would be to wreck the whole ship, for since the linguistic character of religion consists in its pushing at the edge of its area of deepest concern (the story of particular men and of mankind in the case of Christianity), Christianity without an apocalyptic element would no longer be a religion at all.

Because the subject, the limits of whose expression are being strained, is human history, indeed the history of a man set within that of his people, and so also the history of that people, apocalyptic imagery centers in a social vision, "the Kingdom." It is a kingdom of an unusual sort. It is presented first in the parables of the Gospels as like our ordinary life, yet strangely different. In parable after parable, quite ordinary scenes of our historical existence are presented, developed to make a point, and then dropped, with the warning that not all have ears to hear. In short, unambiguous situations are so

developed that they pose a question. What begins fairly
straightforwardly (e.g., "A man had two sons") ends by sending
us away to consider what human faithfulness is. With considerably less restraint, apocalyptic writing likewise pushes out
from the home-field of language about our existence as social
beings in the world, and strains at the edge of that language
to the point of nonsense. The vision of a universal Kingdom
in which there is no death and which brings history itself to an
end is therefore the logical climax to a religious concern for
history!

Let us now develop our analysis by reviewing chronologi-
cally the development of how the Jews and then the Christians
talked of themselves and their history, as they stretched their
language out from its rule-governed base until the rules
almost ceased to govern. Although the talk of Christians
centers in speaking of the man Jesus, its roots lie in speaking of
the people among whom he was born. This people, Israel,
emerges on the historian's scene from a condition of slavery,
with earlier folk traditions that reach back to an Abramic
migration from the east into the land of Canaan. Equally
unambiguously, the escape from slavery gave this people a
sense of their own identity and destiny, and under the leader-
ship of Moses they made their return to the land they understood as destined for them. In time they infiltrated it, drove
out their enemies, and settled down. They had periods of
glory, under David, and periods of affliction, when they were
caught in the power struggles of the larger nations about them.
They saw this wider world as a context for their identity and
destiny as a people; the actions of their neighbors were
aspects of the working out of their own history as a people.
However, a historian might judge such matters differently, and
already we can see the beginning of the process of stretching
discourse about historical events.

Within this context (still keeping close to the least ambiguous
and most clearly rule-governed area of historical language),
during one of Israel's difficult periods, under Roman domina-
tion, Jesus was born. He was a man whose parents were known,

and the dates of his life can be fixed within tolerable limits. Most of his career is unknown, but he appeared in connection with a revolutionary movement led by John the Baptist, began a public life as an itinerant preacher, drawing followers, until finally he was arrested and killed by the Roman authorities as one more insurgent leader of this rebellious and difficult people. Of the man's activities and teachings, we have only what can be deduced from a collection of writings, the earliest of which dates from about a generation after his death, and all of which were written by members of the movement which grew out of some of his followers, in the conviction that the crucified Jesus had appeared to some of them as alive once more. Being all Jews and the followers of the Jew, Jesus, the "Christians" (as they came to be called) kept these writings together with the writings of Israel and saw their own story as part of that older story. Roughly speaking, then, and in the briefest compass, the home-base of Christian discourse begins in the area fixed by the history of Israel, the wider context in which that is set, and the history of Jesus, together with the writings of those who followed him.

From this relatively unambiguous center, the stretching process can be seen to develop, first in the Old Testament. The accounts of Israel's escape from slavery and new sense of identity were pushed out to speaking of an eternal election by that which (or by the One who) ruled all human destiny. And as the Children of Israel understood themselves to have been given their existence as a people by this election, so their sense of the whole natural world as the context of this election led them to recast Near Eastern mythology to tell of the world as having been called into existence solely as the context for their election![11] That is more than exaggeration! That is dancing of the wildest sort along the farthest edge of language.

Considering this background, we are not surprised to find the early followers of Jesus seeing his story as part of this "tall tale" of Israel's election. They stretched their talk of him

11. This stretching process behind the creation stories was worked out in his commentary on *Genesis* by G. von Rad.

until he was called the son of David, indeed Israel itself, the fulfillment of the Law and the prophets, the very embodiment in flesh of the meaning and purpose of Israel's call. And the writings which record the thoughts, ideas, and actions of these earliest Christians were said later to be the very word of eternal truth, the word announcing to the faithful that they too, though born Gentiles, were privileged to have been made younger brothers of that faithful Jew of Nazareth, and thus Jews by adoption, sons of Abraham, grafted into the eternally chosen Israel.

Such an extended use of language as we have described lies just this side of nonsense. Somewhere the applications of these words in such extended usages must break down. Yet we have also seen that as social behavior, language's borders can be pushed out; the conventions can in time be changed. If that comes about, however, it is the result of a social effort, a large enough group of people coming eventually to extend the rules of their language to reach out to a farther frontier. As far as Christianity is concerned, there can be little doubt that this did in fact take place. The early Christians wanted to say more than even their Jewish tradition of language-stretching allowed, and so they came to say things which were not said elsewhere, but which eventually became (among them, at least) rule-governed. The story of the long argument about the rules is the story of Christian theology, which has tried to establish rules for talking along the edge of language and thereby tame the restless frontier and make it rule-governed. For even when they made extensions to rules or made new rules, defining in ecumenical councils that *this* they must and could say together (their "creeds" registering their conventions), whereas no one was to say *that* within their society (*anathema sit*), there was still a limit beyond which language did not and could not go, but against which the religious spirit continually pushed. The final sign of that last limit—the word which stood for saying, "Here we long to say more and know not how," the word that is religion's peculiar way of acknowledging the final limit of its language—is "God." The logic of God, then, is the logic of the edges of language, and the man who says "God" in a serious way is engaging in the farthest extremeties of the linguistic behavior that is religion. There are other forms of walking the borders of language, as we have seen, which do not involve the use of this word. And there are other religions in which this word appears in sections of language other than the historical. To arrive at the edge of speaking of the history of Israel and of the man Jesus, however, and to use the word 'God' at that point is to engage in the discourse of the Christian religion. It was so in the first century and it remains so for a twentieth-century Christian. In order to complete our analysis of the discourse of Christians, therefore, we must now describe how the word 'God' functions as the decisive boundary marker at the edge of their language.

CHAPTER VIII
The Word 'God' as the Limit of Language

We have argued that language, as rule-governed behavior, has limits or edges, and we have tried to draw attention to that use of language which consists in pushing at those limits. This behavior can take various forms, as we have seen, one of which is that of religion. In the Christian religion, this behavior arises from the urge to say the utmost concerning the past and future of Jesus of Nazareth, of his people Israel, and then of others, including the speaker, who consider themselves to be associated with that people. At this point, and around this complex of subjects which we have indicated with the word "history" (used in an already extended sense), Christians use the word 'God.' The logic of 'God,' then, is the logic of the last limit of language. We shall now clarify this logic as it works out for Christianity.

It may seem paradoxical, to say the least, to maintain that the word 'God' as the Christian uses it, marks the final limit of his language. For, surely, it might be objected, 'God' is the word Christians use to *name* a supreme, personal being, who they think exists as the first fact of the universe. Indeed, theism consists just in believing that there is such a being, and surely Christianity is one form of theism? This is the factual interpretation of religious discourse, the first of the three we discussed in Chapter II.

There are certainly those who, calling themselves Christians, believe Christianity to be a form (they may want to say, the ultimate or truest form) of such a theism. I leave it to them to find their own defenses against the attacks of those who have argued in detail the incoherence of such a concept as these theists take 'God' to be. I would add only the point that if 'God' is not a word marking the outer edge of language, then it falls within our clear, regular use of words and must stand the tests of coherence which rule what I should call the great central plains of our talk. If, on the other hand, however, 'God' is conceived of as a word uttered when one wants desperately to say the most that is possible, if its use is the final speech-act at the limit of language, then the categories of coherence employed to attack the theist simply do not apply. The attempt to apply here the distinction between coherence and incoherence is itself incoherent; perhaps this is the source of the total breakdown in communication between the atheist philosopher and the educated contemporary Christian. The one attacks a literal theism which the other also finds unattractive. Indeed, I want to argue that while there have certainly been Christian theists, there has also been at the least an important, at the most the central, strain of Christianity which has consistently refused to allow a use of the word 'God' like that presupposed in the argument between theists and atheists.

If God is not the "object" of a Christian's belief, that before which he stands in awe, then what is? Vernon Pratt argues in a recent article that although religious awe must have some sort of object, the existence of that object is not established just because believers have a feeling of awe.[1]

To illustrate the point, he makes use of a haunting scene from Kenneth Grahame's *The Wind in the Willows* in which the stalwart Mole and his faithful friend Rat, having hunted high and low for the lost baby otter, come to an island in the river. They hear a strange music, and, pushing tremblingly on, they stand transfixed with heads bowed before the god Pan,

1. Vernon Pratt, "Feeling Awed by God," *Mind* (October, 1970), pp. 607-12.

with the baby otter sleeping peacefully at his feet. That awe
is appropriate, Pratt argues, because, by Grahame's arrange-
ment, they are standing in the sacred presence of the awesome
Pan. And religious mystics declare that they are in awe of the
presence of God, not the idea or thought of God. So he who is
awed ought to be able to give, if asked, an answer to the
question, "By what are you awed?" for to be awestruck implies
an awesome something or someone. Pratt's point is, of course,
that it is false to assume, with Rudolf Otto, that the implica-
tion of a presence is in fact evidence for it. If we cannot say
what it is that awes us—and few religious people can give an
account of the object of their awe—then we ought to withdraw
our claim to being awestruck rather than "indulge in onto-
genesis by capitalization and invent a Presence in order to
bear the logical burden which being awestruck drags along
wherever it goes."[2]

The argument seems sound. To be awestruck implies that
there is something of which one stands in awe, and one ought
to be able to say what that is. But has Pratt read Grahame's
story aright? Has his interpretation not been somewhat con-
ditioned by the preconception that a God (whatever that may
be) is the object of awe? Forgotten in this account are the
desperate search, the evident distress of Mole and Rat before
the painful suffering of Otter, the joy at the sight of the little
otter before—yes, before what? "Pan," says Pratt, forgetting
that Grahame mentioned no name. Indeed, Grahame's identi-
fication of the demi-god is subtle. Is Pan there, like a tree, or
have the animals imagined this personification of all that works
to protect them? As the Vision disappears and Mole and Rat
seem unable to recall having seen anything, the reader is left
wondering. Of course there is an object to the awe of the two
small animals: the stillness and beauty of the predawn, and
above all the discovery that the little lost one is not lost, that
he is safe and sound after all the agony of the long search.
They do not take the successful outcome of their hunt as a
matter of course, but as an event before which they are

2. *Ibid.*, p. 612.

rendered almost speechless, their paradoxical and self-contradictory utterances giving way to silence. Such are the occasions which lead men to press on to the limit of rule-governed ways of speaking about finding something that was lost. "For this my son was lost and is found." No, more! And first of all, "He was dead and is alive!" Awe before what can be described in ordinary terms (cf. the average newspaper account of finding a lost child) can also produce extraordinary language.

It is true that mystics say that they are awestruck by the presence of God, not by the idea of God. But the words of mystics are notoriously ambiguous and paradoxical. Taoist mystics remind us that the Tao that can be spoken is not the real Tao. In fact, mystics are the most insistent of all believers that God is ineffable, that all words break down, including their own, in saying (the simple-minded may take this to be their "claim") that they were awestruck by the "presence of God." Mysticism can be of many sorts, but in the Christian tradition, as in any other, there is always an "object" of the mystic's awe. For Christian mystics, that object is the history—Christians would want to say, the strange, awesome history—of a people escaped from slavery into communal identity, a history which culminates in the history of one man who was the totally faithful Jew, and which was interrupted, they would say, but not finished, by his death. To regard "God" as a name for the object of awe depends upon too limited a view of language. It forgets or fails to notice another part of our language-in-use: speaking at its edge, in which the word "God" marks the point at which the religious man has come up against the final limit of what he can say about the object of his concern.

Without a doubt there are religionists of the sort that Vernon Pratt and Kai Nielson and Antony Flew have in mind. We have all of us met them at one time or another. They come to our doors selling strange tracts. They are the ones in every religion who claim exclusive "orthodoxy." They are those whom we may properly call doctrinal literalists.

They are, however, naïve about language, treating the crucial terms of religion as if they were just further words on the broad home-field of our speaking. God, in this view, may be an exceedingly exceptional individual, but he is at least an individual. That much is clear, they say. Or if some cannot say that, then they suggest that we can at least say unambiguously that God is Being itself.[3] In any case, they feel it appropriate to look for some unambiguous thing to say, thereby betraying that their teaching, their doctrine, lies in the literal realms well within the borders of language.

It takes no atheist to see the absurdity of the position of doctrinal literalists. Christian theologians from as wide a historical and philosophical spread as Aquinas and Barth have seen the absurdity themselves and have argued that the word 'God' is not to be brought into such a simple juxtaposition with our relatively clear ways of speaking as the doctrinal literalists suppose. The discovery of modern philosophers that the word 'God,' when taken as the name of a supposed being and as a designation whose "reference range" may be fixed, is an incoherent word takes only the first step along a road which sophisticated believers have long been traveling. If philosophers want to understand the logic of 'God,' they could do worse than drop their preconceptions and theories, and simply look with care and see how the word is used.

Language is a learned behavior, and so is language used on its frontiers. One learns from those who have already become masters of the language to say certain things in a certain context. The Christian use of the word 'God' is also a learned use, and therefore it can also be mislearned, or misunderstood. The methods of instruction practiced in the communities which use this word (Sunday school—also much popular

3. The difference between literalists of the simplest sort, whose statements about God may be judged false rather than incoherent, and literalists of a more sophisticated sort, whose use of the word 'God' is incoherent is considerable, but it is not important to my argument. The distinction was clearly drawn by T. R. Miles in his *Religion and the Scientific Outlook* (London: Allen & Unwin, 1959) under the headings "literal theism" and "qualified literal theism."

preaching and many popular hymns) give no reason to expect that persons mildly exposed to Christianity will get it right, for not many of their teachers seem to have it right. We might as well expect a sound appreciation of our artistic heritage to be passed on by the teaching done by some volunteer groups of young ladies who perform a service (?) for museums comparable to that performed by some Sunday school teachers. Overhearing their commentary on paintings with which one is familiar can be a bit unsettling, to say the least. Realizing that the peculiarly Christian use of this word is unusual and that it has been badly taught in the past, many churches have been in recent years revising catechisms and reordering their whole conception of "Christian Education."

If there can be a proper use for Christians of 'God,' there can also be more than one improper use. The most widespread misuse is to think of this word as naming someone, a word which is supposed to refer to, or name, its object. This is simply the factual interpretation we discussed in Chapter II.

As we have seen, not all words refer to, or name, something. The word "mind" is an obvious example. When we speak of someone having a fine mind, of having something on his mind, or in mind, the word does not in fact refer to an organ, or a place, or anything else. If mind were to become my preoccupation, so that I claimed to be amazed by the human mind, this awe would not have a tangible or localizable thing as its object. I should be saying, rather, that I was amazed by what people said and did. Although to say that I was amazed or overawed by Israel's God would be quite different, it would be a mistake here, too, to go looking for this 'God' or for his evidences, just as it would be wrong in the other case to look for a mind with a powerful microscope or X-ray machine. In both cases the evidence that counts lies in the circumstances in which the word is used. In the case of Israel's God, the evidence is that which Israel has presented: the history of the people, the very survival of Israel at all (considering its tragic history), and such faithfulness as Israel has been able to muster.

Naturally, no one has to be amazed by the human mind, and

no one has to be overawed by Israel's God. Mole and Rat, likewise, could have taken the finding of the little otter as the most matter-of-fact occurrence in the world. But if a man is overawed before what men do, or before the history of Israel, or before the preservation of a helpless baby otter, then the difference between that person and one who is not struck in the same way is not that the one is incoherent and confused and the other thinking and speaking clearly. Of course, the one is not speaking clearly and the other is, for the one is walking the edges of language and the other is not. The issue, then, is not a matter of who is being logical, or who is handling language properly, but with which *part* of language each is involved.

In order to understand the Christian, as distinct from the theistic, use of the word 'God,' it is appropriate to turn to its employment in the classic creeds, since these have been regarded by most Christians as a guideline for what they ought to say. In the creeds the word 'God' first occurs in connection with the words "one," "father," "almighty," and "maker of heaven and earth." Now it is possible to say that these words are predicates "of God," and that they are claims which Christians make "about God." It is, if you will, "God-talk"— an expression appearing in several important recent books of theology.[4] To take "God-talk" as equivalent to "talk of or about God," however, is to beg the whole question right from the start. These so-called "claims" are in fact other words used together with the word 'God.' The literalists and other persons who are unaware of the frontiers of language and who think that all words work in all circumstances as they do on its broad, central plains assume that oneness, fatherhood, omnipotence, and the rest, are modifiers of a substantive, 'God.' These are considered to be, to use an old and misleading term, attributes of God. But if we are on the right track in placing distinctively religious discourse at language's

4. John Macquarrie, *God Talk* (London: S.C.M. Press, 1967); and the subtitle of Gilkey's *Naming the Whirlwind* is "The Renewal of God-Talk."

edges, then the literalists have the matter backward. These so-called attributes are not qualities belonging to an object; they are, rather, the subjects about which the Christian tries to say more than our ordinary linguistic conventions allow. He wants, indeed, not only to stretch those conventions, but to go to the very limit of the extended conventions of his own religious community. Therefore, he uses a word that marks the final limit for the religious community: 'God.'

He wants to say the most that could possibly be said about fatherhood, drawing upon the rich use of that word developed during Israel's history. He wants to speak of a loving father, employing every image he can form of a father perfect in all things. He wants to push on and say that we men are together as brothers might be imagined to be, had they one perfect father. But when he has said all that, he remains dissatisfied with his words, as though the last word on this matter had not yet been said. In order to grasp that final limit, therefore, the Christian sometimes cries, "Father!" (a balancing act on the outer edge of language initiated by Jesus of Nazareth).

He wants, further, to say something more and other about power than our usual language allows. When he speaks of power, therefore, he extends the rules to the breaking-point: "almighty" and "omnipotent" have no application in the world we know. In Christian usage, however, those words do not simply mean, "a great deal more of the sort of power we know already." The "power" that is awesome for the Christian is tied up with the word "father," and both terms are linked with the figure of Jesus of Nazareth. Jesus' story presents the image of what it is to have the "father" Christians speak of, and his humble way in the world is what they mean by "power," "almighty power." The logic of "the power of God" is hardly that of "the power of the king," but it does have a logic: that of frontier-language, near the final limit marked by the word 'God.'

The Christian says that this "fatherhood" and this strange powerless "omnipotence" is "for us" and can be known to be for us "in Jesus Christ," because this Jesus was "raised from the dead." He wants to say the most that can be said about the way in which one man's life can either give us a clue to the meaning of life or influence other men to change their understanding of life. Concerning this man, his birth, life, and death, and concerning the continuance of his history, he says in effect, "This is too important for ordinary discourse; I want to go farther than we usually go in speaking of great men." Dissatisfied with every other approach to the limit of such talk he adopts the behavior he has learned from his religious community. He has learned at this point to say "God."

So one could continue, with the forgiveness of sins, the church, and life in which no man's history is lost, ending with that final righteousness, that final putting-in-order, which is expressed by the biblical word 'judgment.' These are all matters of which the Christian could almost as well remain silent. However, he has learned this other form of linguistic behavior, which is to go as far as he can, to stumble at the edge of utter nonsense, and then to cry, "God!"

The literalists on both sides, theists and atheists, simply miss what is going on. Having too narrow a view of the workings of our language, being too much preoccupied with what we can do with language near its center, they do not notice there is more to our use of words than is dreamed of in their philosophy. In order to reach a better understanding of "God-talk," we do not need an alternative to attentiveness to the workings of language, nor some other method which "goes beyond language." What is needed is just that minute attention to words and how they work which modern philosophy has taught us to respect. Without this attention, theists and atheists alike mistake walking the edges of language for inept or misguided center-field behavior. The wobbles of those who balance on language's outer edge are taken by them to be a sign of clumsiness. Both think that some *thing* is named or referred to when the Christian says "God," and that despite the long history of Christian objections that this is neither a name nor a description nor a word having a specific object as its reference.

Theists themselves are primarily responsible for contemporary confusion about the word 'God.' They have used the word as though it belonged in that relatively clear stretch of language in which concepts can be used coherently and incoherently, as that distinction is made near the center of our linguistic activity. Those among them who also call themselves Christians, however, ignore the workings of language within their own religious tradition. To illustrate that further, we may consider what goes on linguistically in that story which is as crucial for Christianity as it is for Judaism: the story of Moses and the Israelites before Mount Sinai (Exodus 19ff.).

As they came to tell this story about themselves and this event, the Hebrews at Sinai split into two camps, with Moses and "the faithful" on one side, and the unfaithful on the other. The issue which divided them was how they should speak of their recent escape from Egypt. This issue became focused in what was later called the First Commandment: "I am *YHWH* [this supposed 'name' was never spoken by them], your *Elohim* [should we translate this as 'God'—as if that would make it any clearer?], who brought you out of the land of Egypt, out of the house of bondage. You shall have no other *Elohim* before [or beside] me" (Exodus 20: 2-3). With these words Israel confessed the utter centrality of the Exodus as that event which made them a people. With maddening circumlocution they persisted in giving thanks for that event solely in terms of the event itself: the rescuer from Egypt is the rescuer from Egypt, the redeemer from slavery is the redeemer from slavery, never to be named or defined otherwise. On this event their very identity depended, as they saw it. (No wonder they found themselves stumbling at the edge of language!) The question was whether all would agree to speak of their deliverance in this way.

That this is a fair description of the issue is clear from the way in which they told the story, for their story recounts that large numbers of them, almost from the moment of their escape, began to give the credit for this happening to something other than the unnameable deliverer—to what could be

named and spoken of unambiguously. They began to say it
was Moses who had led them out, first for worse and then for
better. When Moses retreated from this praise and disappeared
on the mountain, they persisted in keeping things definable
and produced a golden calf as their rescuing *Elohim* until
Moses returned. The issue which divided the two camps was
how to speak, where to ascribe the credit for this adventure:
to the unnamed, or to Moses as their leader and (we may add,
in the light of subsequent events) to themselves who had such
a leader.

As one considers the later history of Israel, it becomes clear
why this story is central to their tradition and why the First
Commandment to honor no other God is the first of the
Mosaic commandments and was to remain central. It is likewise central in the history of that other people, the Christians,
who regarded themselves as adopted sons of Abraham, by
right of having an elder brother who was (as they saw it)
Abraham's truest son. The choice before Mount Sinai was the
decisive choice for Israel. Moses and the faithful after him
looked back to that rescue from slavery, knew that they wanted
intensely to give thanks for it, but refused to settle for any of
the unambiguous answers that they might have given about
"whom" they had to thank. They refused to give the credit to
Moses, refused to take the credit themselves, would not
ascribe it to changes in Egyptian politics or policies for dealing
with slaves, and so they were pushed to giving credit to an
unnameable, whom they defined only as "the one who" (this
is language for persons stretched to the limits) delivered them
from slavery. They felt that if they had come into existence by
the hand of this *Elohim*, then by this same *Elohim* they would
endure. To trust in their army, to wish for a king, to take their
place on the plane of history as just one more nation like all
the others was excluded for them by their having no *Elohim*
before that which had rescued them from slavery. To be Israel
was to walk or stand humbly and in awe at the limit of what
can be said in the face of the righteousness and mercy which
they saw in this redemption from Egyptian slavery.

Throughout Israel's history, however, there recurred the voice of those whom Israel regarded as the unfaithful, saying simply that it was Moses who had rescued them. This voice was regarded as that of the unfaithful because its very clarity tended to undercut their sense of being defined only by their deliverance. The logic and the historical consequences of this are not hard to see. If the credit is not reserved to the inexpressible (except by speaking of the deliverance again), then it can be assigned to Moses. At first the unfaithful said that he had led them out of Egypt in reproach, for they thought they would only die in the wilderness. But when better times finally came, when they had moved into Canaan, settled down, and begun to feel at home, they or their unfaithful descendants said, in effect, "It was surely we who pulled off that escape, our leader and our own tough Hebrew character that brought us through. We did it before and we can do it again!" When, centuries later, invasions from the north threatened them with slavery again, the cry was for strengthening the army, for an alliance with Egypt, for military escalation, just like any other nation. Their leader, their own stubborn character, their king, or their army, became their *Elohim*, their self-definers, to the horror of Amos and (in later times) Isaiah and Jeremiah. Their origin betrayed and the First Commandment broken, their existence as a peculiar people was threatened and almost cut off. The issue presented in the Sinai story remained the central issue of Israel's history.

I have interpreted the Sinai story and the recurring issue of faithfulness for Israel and Christianity linguistically. According to this interpretation, the issue has been whether to go to the limit of language in speaking of the "object" of worship and thanksgiving. If Israel's temptation was to stop short of language's frontiers, Christianity has suffered from an opposite temptation: to think that it was possible to go to the outer edge and still speak clearly at that point, presuming to offer definitions of God. If the threat to Israel's religion was humanism, then the danger for Christianity has been gnosticism.

It could be objected against this description of the lingustic
issue for Judaism and Christianity that, since the very story of
Sinai tells of God speaking, it confronts us with the problem
of revelation from outside the sphere of human language and
thereby shows that religion is from the beginning committed
to presuming to go beyond the limits of language. Moreover,
the prophets began their proclamations by asserting, "thus
says the Lord." Surely this language pretends it has no limits.
It must be conceded that the Sinai story does say that God
spoke to Moses, and the prophets do claim that "the Lord"
spoke to them. The question is: How shall we describe such
language? If we make the mistake of thinking this language to
be precisely governed by the rules which control "John said to
me," we shall find ourselves on the slippery path to theism.
That Christian thinkers and writers have frequently made this
mistake is hardly to be denied. We need not insist on the hope-
lessness of that slide, which was demonstrated in connection
with Wittgenstein's remark about not being able to understand
a lion who talked. To take that path is to forget both how Israel
talked of its deliverance, and also the fact that Christian theologians have known that their words "about God" were not
at all "about God," that no definition of God in fact defines
God, that God is ineffable. I myself once argued that the word
"God" was meaningless, that it was dead[5]—an example of the
same mistake about language which we are discussing here.
The mistake is to think that the word 'God' either falls well
within the edges of language, where religious claims about God
would be meaningful but would appear to be false, or else lies
outside language altogether. It seems evident to me now that
the word had never had much life in either of these foreign
soils. Planted in its own ground, however, right on, and marking, the boundary of language, the word can be as alive and
flourishing today as in the past. If saying "God" is an acknowledgment that one has come to the end of language, if it is a

5. Van Buren, *The Secular Meaning of the Gospel* (New York: The
Macmillan Company, 1963; London: S.C.M. Press, 1963; Penguin,
1968).

religious way of indicating that one longs to say all that could possibly be said on some matter of great concern, then that is a role which lies just barely but legitimately within our language.

This placing accounts for the puzzling paradoxes in the way Christian thinkers of the past have used the word "God." Well-established theological conventions, such as that God is personal but not a person, that he cannot be known "in himself" (this idea dates from an age in which it was thought that things generally could be known "in themselves"), that it is strictly speaking improper to say that God exists as it is also to say that he does not exist, that for God essence and existence are identical—all these ideas take on another color when viewed as attempts to deal with a word that marks the border of language. In its own way, however, this older theological tradition was saying that an interpretation of God along the lines of straightforward "minimal" (or even maximal) theism simply will not do.

Theologians would not have said these things, however, if Christians had not also used the word 'God' as if it were as clear as "John" or "a storm." The modern discussions between theists and atheists would hardly have developed had not large numbers of Christians in effect made "graven images" of God, not unlike those proscribed in the so-called Second Commandment. That is to say, they treated "God" as an entity for which definitions could be given, or at least for which a definition would make sense if a proper one could be formulated. They attempted to imagine, picture, think about, and speak of God and became doctrinal literalists—in a word: theists.

Theism is an almost inevitable product of the marriage of Christianity with Western culture, which was consummated in the Constantinian era and which is denounced by many Christians today under the name of "Christendom." That submission to the surrounding culture included the adoption of the widespread cultural habit (only recently called into question) of thinking that every noun stands for something and that consequently the word 'God' must stand for a bearer of which it is the name. If philosophers have only in recent decades been able to work themselves loose from this habit, it is no surprise that uneducated Christians in the past did not lead the way. Yet if any modern observers had bothered to notice how at least some Christians were using the word 'God,' they would have seen that here was an exception to what was thought to be a general rule. Even the celebrated proposal of Anselm, that 'God' is "that than which nothing greater can be conceived," might have given the clue, had not Anselm and his opponents both thought that the issue was the possibility of a logical demonstration of God's necessary existence.[6] When we consider other thinkers who insisted that God cannot be spoken of adequately, that we can have no direct knowledge of him because he is quite apart from all we can know, touch, think of, imagine, or define, we can see that evidence has been around for some time that at least some of what men do with words is other than naming things and making "statements." In the light of this evidence, the so-called revolution in philosophy appears to have had precedents.

We are not denying that many Christians did use the word 'God' as lying well within language's borders, and Christianity has indeed paid deservedly for using a border-marker to plow in the center of its fields. Moreover, the damage is still being done by those who persist in the linguistic ignorance of doctrinal literalism. Nowhere do the difficulties of this persistence come out more clearly than the way in which Christian thinkers in some quarters speak of transcendence. That is to say, they use this word as if it were *not* a border-marker like the word 'God.' The word, with its inescapable spatial imagery, suggests that something goes on out beyond, or comes in from beyond, the limits of our language. Once more, the image

6. The issue that still calls for more subtle consideration is whether "that than which nothing greater can be conceived" is in fact conceivable. If the phrase is really meant to do duty for the word 'God' as the Christian uses it, then will it not mark the limit of conceivability? In which case it will hardly be itself conceivable in any ordinary sense of that word. But of that another time, perhaps.

which lurks behind the word "transcendence" is that of language as a cage which can be opened by this word that enters from the outside (on the assumption that an outside is just as possible as an inside). Such a use of the word "transcendence" is tied irrevocably to a view of language that is not simply out-of-date, but false: a misdescription of the workings of our language.

Christianity would have to pay an exceedingly high price if it were tied to that misconception of language, for if it abandoned its historically nourished speech on language's border, its use of the word 'God,' for this seemingly less offensive word "transcendence," it would lose the only linguistic placing it has ever had. It would then become one more activity on the great plains of language, one more form of linguistic behavior that knows nothing of language's edges. It might try to compete on those terms, but we have seen enough of this in religious literalism already to suspect that few educated persons would long accept such a sacrifice of intelligence as this position requires. However, the survival and even growth of literalistic variants of Christianity suggests that among the unsophisticated, both theism and a central plains use of the word "transcendence" may have a considerable future ahead of them.

Those who have toyed with a religious use of "transcendence" have perhaps not seen the proper logic of 'God.' They seem to have failed to see the word 'God' as a speech-act acknowledging the limits of speech, and turned elsewhere for a word that would do justice to their longing to say more than is possible with a clear use of words. As rational men they have perhaps felt uneasy with the stumbling gait of walking language's frontier, have also wanted to use something more than the vague word "mystery," and yet do something more than taking the way of silence. It may be hoped that further reflection on the logic of 'God' will offer a better way. If it is realized that religious utterances are more adequately described as language at the limit of its use than as assertions, then it may be seen that the word "transcendence" could also be used as an

edge-marker. Since such a use would not pretend to "go
beyond" or even to "point beyond" language, however, the
spatial connotation of the word makes it a misleading synonym
for 'God.'

We saw in Chapter II that theists and atheists agree that
religion is about the facts, and that God is the first fact of all.
On the basis of the alternative description developed in these
pages, we can grant that Christians do make much of the facts
of the history of Israel and the Israelite Jesus. It is precisely in
the "making much of," however, that religion consists, in
pushing to the limits of what can be said of this history and
still longing to say more. At this point Christians use the word
'God,' saying such things as "God did this thing," "In Christ
God was reconciling the world to himself," and "Here we see
the love of God." The linguistically naïve may call these "statements," but we have tried to show that "statement" is an exceedingly inadequate description of the speech-act in question.

We may also say that as the prime case of a Christian's
arrival at the frontier of language, 'God' is indeed the primary
fact for the Christian, the primary linguistic fact. But we do
not say it is the primary fact *only* in a linguistic sense, for
language and life are too much of a piece for us to abstract
a believer's word, the one about which he cares most, the word
which is most "his own," from other ways in which we speak
about that man's life and existence. Indeed, then, God is the
supreme fact for the Christian (though hardly in the sense
which atheists and theists give to these words).

One of the best-known challenges made to the theist's position was made some years ago by Antony Flew in his parable
of two explorers. The parable has been much discussed, and
it may be appropriate to conclude this section of my argument
by seeing how the parable would have to be told if it had had
to do with a Christian rather than a theist. It will be recalled
that two explorers come to a clearing in the jungle. One says
that a gardener (the theist's God?) comes to take care of the
garden whereas the other, seeing the wildness of even the
clearing, maintains that there is no gardener. Neither dis-

agrees as to the amount of order and disorder they see in the clearing. After they set their watches and patrol with blood-hounds, and no evidence of an intruder is found, still the believing explorer maintains that an invisible, totally illusive gardener comes, to which the skeptic replies that there is no difference between the work of such a gardener and that of an imaginary gardener, or even of no gardener at all.

Now suppose that the believing explorer (for are all believers alike?) were a contemporary Western Christian aware of the "linguistic turn" in philosophy, knowledgeable about his tradition, and also aware of the way in which Christian thinkers were reforming catechisms today in order to correct misunder-standings of that tradition. He comes upon the clearing, and let us say (for we cannot ignore this point) that the clearing reminds him of the story of Eden, or the escape of Israel from the wilderness, or the promise of the prophet that the wilder-ness shall burst forth in flowers. He might well say, "Look! A veritable garden, the work of a loving hand!" for he might use such a biblical image to do the work of the word 'God.' That is, he feels strongly and therefore wants to say more about gardens and the wilderness than standard rules allow. The other explorer, standing flat in the great plains of lan-guage and thinking that his companion (although perhaps suffering momentarily from too much exertion) is also stand-ing there, answers, "There is no gardener." And how shall the Christian answer then? I suggest that as sound an answer as he could give under the circumstances would go something like this: "All right, have it your way! There is no gardener and this is no garden, and we aren't explorers either, but just two collections of biological tissue and psychological drives pushed by our environment and heredity, and there is really, as you say, nothing else to be said!" But he might also add, "But as for me, I want to talk in other words also about how we find ourselves here at this moment, and to say more about this place. Indeed, I care so much about where we came from and where we are going and the beauty of this spot, that I can scarcely find words for it. So I persist in saying that some

wonderful Gardener cares for this place." I will not presume
to guess how either one will continue the conversation, but it
is evident that it cannot continue as in the original parable.[7]
But then the original parable leaves no room for that use
of words which we have been describing.

Let those who find themselves talking like Flew's believing
explorer attempt to meet the challenge which Flew developed
out of his parable. I have no interest in coming to their
defense. I think it is fair to judge, however, that not all contemporary educated Christians will be among that number.
I suggest that many of them will be found using the word
'God' at the limits of language and therefore untouched by
the parable of the two explorers.

7. The conversation cannot continue as in Flew's original parable,
   that is, but it might come closer to that of the parable of the two
   gardeners which Flew borrowed (and distorted) from John Wisdom's "Gods."

CHAPTER IX
Religion, Morals, and Metaphysics

The discourse of Christians can be misunderstood in more than one way. When the limits of language are forgotten or ignored, as is the case in a theistic interpretation of Christianity, such words as 'God,' "transcendent," "ultimate," and "eternal" are thought to refer to that which lies beyond human life and experience. Religion, so misunderstood, consequently presumes to go beyond language, rather than be content to hover right at the limits of what we are able to say.

It is also possible to misunderstand the discourse of Christians in the opposite way: by stopping short of the frontiers of language and locating it somewhere within the broad area of our relatively unambiguous use of words. A primitive way of doing this is to take biblical anthropomorphism literally, moving God-talk right into the range of our ordinary discussion of historical events. The result is that God becomes an identifiable historical personage, who seems to have unfortunately become decreasingly active with the rise of Western science and the increase of mass education. An educated Christian today will not be attracted by that move, but he may be tempted by the more sophisticated refusal to go to the edges of language, which we described in Chapter II as the moral interpretation of religious discourse. In that interpretation, it will be recalled, Christianity is conceived as a moral commitment and its characteristic utterances are analyzed as assertions of an intention to follow a certain way of life. The affirmation that God is love is taken to be the expression of an intention to behave lovingly in the light of the Christian story.[1] According to a similar interpretation, when a Christian says that Jesus is Lord, he is expressing or commending his commitment to a way of seeing the world, to a perspective oriented to the figure of Jesus of Nazareth.[2]

This interpretation misunderstands religion in a manner opposite to that of theism, because its way of ignoring the borders of language is to stay safely within them. If theism depends upon an over-confidence in the possibility of surmounting language, the moral interpretation of Christian discourse arises from an unnecessary timidity before the full possibilities of our ways of speaking. It fears to venture in those realms of language where the light is dim, the shadows are confusing, and matters are unclear.

The avoidance of the frontiers of language is not incidental to the moral interpretation; it is central to its thesis. The clue to the grounds for avoidance is the word "empirical"—a word which has no small status in our present world, and for good reason. What we can come to terms with, find out about, test, and make use of, by means of our senses, is of great importance to sentient creatures. The moral interpretation assumes that if religion is important, it must matter in that same realm where we can distinguish clearly between what can and what cannot be seen, heard, and touched. It is no accident, therefore, that Braithwaite began his famous essay, "An Empiricist's View of the Nature of Religious Belief," with the demand for clarity. There are, he said, "three classes of statement whose method of truth-value testing is in general clear: statements about particular matters of empirical fact, scientific hypotheses and other general empirical statements, and the logically necessary statements of logic and mathematics." Finding that

1. As in Braithwaite's "An Empiricist's View of the Nature of Religious Belief."
2. As in van Buren's *The Secular Meaning of the Gospel* (New York: The Macmillan Company, 1963).

religious utterances fall within none of these classes, Braithwaite's concern for clarity leads him to look to moral statements, which, although not empirically verifiable, are at least
clear if they are taken as prescriptions. Religion can also be
made clear if we understand the man who says, "God is love"
to be saying that he intends to follow the path of love.

The meaning of moral "statements" (conceived as announce-
ments of intention) is as clear as those of the other three
classes, if meaning is identical with use (and this is the theory
of meaning to which Braithwaite committed himself in his
essay). But whose use does Braithwaite have in mind here?
The man who says that God is love may have his own idea
of what he is doing when he speaks those words. The empiricist who overhears him, however, may have a different idea
about what the utterance amounts to for him, the empiricist,
regardless of what the religious man may have thought he was
doing. If the empiricist judges that the religious man is affirming a moral intention in empirical terms and calls that the
empirical use of the utterance, he has no right to call it *the*
use. The use that I make of what another man says, regardless
of the use his words have for him (leaving aside all the per-
plexing confusions of the *use-of-words-in-the-language* and the
rather different *use-of-sentences* and other more complex utterances), will hardly pass without comment as *the* use of that
utterance. What I make of another person's utterances may
indeed differ from what he makes of them, yet if there is to be
such a thing as language, there has to be some agreement in
these matters. It is not proper to talk about "the use" unless
there is some minimal agreement between the speaker and the
hearer about what is going on between them when certain
words are said in certain ways. Unless the workings of language are to become quite arbitrary, and language is to cease
to be a conventional matter, the description of the use of an
utterance ought in principle to be something in which speaker
and hearer can agree, even when they cannot share in making
that use their own. Thus if the religious man says (as many
have suspected he would and should say) that of course his

utterance implies his commitment to the way of love, but that
expressing this commitment is only part—and not the most
distinctive part—of what he is doing in speaking thus, then
the "use" of his "statement" has not been adequately described by the moral interpretation.

We can only applaud the desire to achieve all possible
clarity in describing the workings of religious discourse, but
we must protest against a translation of the believer's utterance that has a similar clarity. No paradoxes, no puzzles, no
ambiguities remain in the resulting affirmation of intention.
No word need be applied in an extended or doubtful way. All
works smoothly according to well-agreed rules. In short, edge-
talk has been replaced by center-field talk, and it is maintained
that its *use*, its function, has in no way been changed! If we
are at all correct in seeing the so-called affirmations of religious
persons as cases of frontier-talk, and if that behavior (as we
have described it) is characteristic of religion, then it follows
that a translation of religious utterances into moral assertions
is simply inadequate, for it ignores that distinctive feature.

This is not to argue that Christianity has nothing to do with
morality. Quite the contrary. A moral interpretation of
religion is on the right track, but it should travel that track
to its end. In seeing Christianity as a certain sort of morality,
Braithwaite was following Matthew Arnold, who argued, as
we have seen, that biblical religion is concerned primarily and
emphatically with *conduct*. That is sound enough—as far as it
goes. A "Christianity" not in every point concerned with
human conduct, in the widest sense, would not be Christianity.

Yet morality and religion are not the same. Arnold saw
the difference as one of degree, religion being morality
"heightened" by emotion and the imagination. At some point,
however, differences of degree become differences in kind.
The differences of degree between roller skates and a super-
sonic aircraft, for example, or between a headache and death,
are so great as to be better described as differences of kind.
The difference between the language of morals and language

on its frontiers, we would suggest, is more than a matter of degree: they are two rather different linguistic patterns of behavior.

Braithwaite did distinguish between religion and morality. He made the entertainment of a religious story the feature which differentiates religion from morality. However, even if we improve on this and make the story the source and corrective of the moral principles which the Christian intends to pursue, as suggested earlier, we should have to insist that the "entertainment" would have to be of the strongest sort for morality to become religion. The religious man feels so intensely about that story that he speaks quite differently about it from the way a moral man speaks about principles. Consequently, we need a more accurate word than "entertain," in order to describe correctly the difference between morality and religion.

Whether we accept Braithwaite's or some other analysis of the language of morals, it seems evident that morality consists in acting and living according to moral principles, and doing so under the guidance of moral reasoning. Starting from his moral principles and information concerning the relevant circumstances, the moral person tries to reason his way through to the course of action or the moral judgment at which he arrives. Insofar as any of us are moral beings, we do this sort of thinking, in small matters as well as in more important ones, day in and day out. We may do this so carelessly that we hardly give attention to how well we have reasoned. Yet surely Arnold was right in saying that at least three-fourths of what makes up our lives is conduct, and in most of this conduct, we can usually give some sort of answer, if not always a very good one, to the question: What are your reasons for thinking you ought, or ought not, to do that?

In living a moral life, however, a man need never come anywhere near the edges of language. Indeed, if a man wants to think clearly about moral choices, he will have every reason to steer clear of the limits to which the application of words can be so stretched as to approach nonsense. Normally,

morality and the moral life take place well within the working
ranges of the rules for the use of words.

Religion, on the other hand, or at least the Christian
religion, takes its point of logical *departure*, if I may put it so,
from moral concerns. That is to say, just that area of life with
which morality is concerned, the actions and interactions of
men in history and in society about which a story can be told,
is the area with which religious discourse is connected. The
connection lies not in reasoning about these matters on the
basis of moral principles, however, but in extending to the
limits this way of speaking. Consequently we may say that
religious discourse is moral discourse stretched almost beyond
recognition. Arnold was not altogether unaware of this
relationship, but his definition of religion as "morality tinged
with emotion" has usually been quoted out of context (as
Braithwaite noticed). The phrase hardly does justice to
Arnold's view. Morality is not just tinged, it is thoroughly
stained before it becomes religion. We would shift the ground
slightly but importantly, however, and say, rather, that
religious discourse is strained and stretched moral discourse.
And if moral discourse is already anchored in the strained
historical discourse of the biblical writings, we have a reasonably accurate description of the relationship between religion
and morality in Christianity.

On this basis, we could say that "It is wrong to kill" is the
language of morals. Religion, in addition to calling this a
divine commandment, stretches on to say that it is wrong even
to be angry! Similarly, a moral principle of benevolence is
pushed in religion to the nearly (or actually?) absurd demand
to love our enemies and bless those who curse us! In short,
morality is of such vital concern to the Christian that he wants
to speak of it in an extraordinary way. He pushes on to a
command to be perfect, as God is perfect—and at this point
we hardly know it as morality at all. If morality serves to guide
conduct, how can such a commandment be applied?

Religion being to morality as the frontiers of language are
to firmly rule-governed talk, it is not surprising that each

should find its own appropriate literary form. For morality, it is the essay or treatise, suitable for reasoned discussion. For religion, as we have seen, it is a story, a dramatic rendering of history. Christians have encountered unnecessary difficulties whenever they have taken their story to be a collection of propositions, for example, or a collection of historical evidence and reasoned arguments, or even a message. The "systematic ambiguity" of a story is a far more appropriate vehicle for the ambiguities inherent in language at its borders.[3]

In sum, when the language of morals is pushed to its limits, it is properly speaking no longer the language of morals. It has given way to talk on the frontier. It is no more the language of morals than "God raised Jesus from the dead" is the language of history. We can aim for all possible clarity in the philosophical (not religious) task of describing the workings of religious discourse, but the language whose use we are trying to be clear about is not itself clear. If we transpose it into clear terms, it will no longer be itself or do the job it did. The speech-acts of religion do not merely announce an intention to behave in a certain way, even when such an intention may be gathered from them. These acts are an altogether different piece of our behavior.

Christianity does indeed stand in the most intimate linguistic and practical relationship to morality, but the relationship has moral dangers. Christianity is indeed a way of life, only the Christian would not put it that way. He would say it is *the* life, the more abundant life, eternal life! It is life that presses on to what is more alive than life! It is life with God! And of course, speaking in this wild way, the Christian will always be in danger of pressing on so far, of stretching langauge so hard, that he no longer speaks understandably to our life here and now. Although I think this is an avoidable danger, it can lead to a corruption of Christianity in which religion indeed becomes an opiate. I might add that since in

3. On this, see Louis Hammann, "The Structure and Function of Religious Stories," unpublished dissertation, Temple University, Philadelphia, Pa.

our century Christianity has finally been cast adrift from its too willing anchorage in the harbor of governmental policy, it could scarcely in our time become an opiate of the *people* again, but only of its adherents.

The danger is unavoidable, however, in any religion that allows, however uneasily, a place for mystics. Christians have been generally apprehensive about mysticism, which, linguistically speaking, is a case of concentrating on the edges of language to such an extent that one forgets what part of language is being stretched to the utmost. However, since mysticism is an extreme form of what is genuine in religion, it will endure as long as religion does.

If we rightly understand the logic of language used near its limits, therefore, we can allow mysticism to be a genuine part of religion without concluding that religion will distract men from the center of our daily life, as Bonhoeffer feared. Bonhoeffer's prison letters (which have become the single most influential writings for contemporary, educated Christians) argue that God is not to be found on life's fringes or in man's extremity, but in the center of life and in man's capabilities.[4] It was just there, right in the midst of our most ordinary concerns, that Bonhoeffer wanted to say more than we commonly say. (Not that he always said "God" at such points; for Bonhoeffer advocated silence and an arcane discipline.) Bonhoeffer's concern for God at the center of life, however, conflicts in no way with the description of the use of the word "God" as marking the border of language. The fact that men speak at the edges of language has no necessary connection with the linguistic and existential focus of their particular religion. Such speaking could proceed from any sector of our talk, as we have argued all along. Bonhoeffer believed the focal center of Christianity is our daily life, our history, and our social, political, economic involvement with our fellows and the world around us. It is right there, then, that the Christian wants to push out

4. Published in English under the title *Letters and Papers from Prison* (London: S.C.M. Press, 1953; New York: The Macmillan Company, 1967; enlarged edition, 1972).

the frontiers of what can be said. There is where he "finds God."

The moral interpretation of religious discourse takes as its initial point of departure the narrow base of the verification principle. Finding that the principle cannot be applied to religious utterances, it concludes that they are not about the world. Behind the conclusion there lies an assumption which was questioned by the third, or quasi-metaphysical, interpretation. The assumption is that the world can be adequately and exhaustively described in statements which are in principle empirically falsifiable. It is assumed that there is no other way to say anything about our situation. This assumption is at least open to question. We may agree that empirically falsifiable statements are one of our important ways of talking of our world. The question remains, however, whether we have other ways of saying what is the case with our world and ourselves.

Let us direct the question to the instance of religious utterances; we have described them as language used at its borders. When a man speaks in this way, may he be said, at the least, to imply something about what is the case with the world in which he finds himself? Does the use of edge-language, as we meet it in the Christian religion, for example, commit the speaker to holding identifiable beliefs about our human situation and its context, beliefs that could properly be called either true or false? The quasi-metaphysical interpretation of religious discourse gives an affirmative answer to this question. For reasons of my own and with careful qualification, I would agree. What then are the beliefs to which a man is committed by using the frontier language of Christianity, and in what sense can this commitment be expressed in affirmations which are true or false?

The first judgment about ourselves and our situation to which the Christian is committed is that we are linguistic beings in a linguistically apprehended world. Within this framework, he is committed to the belief that our language has limits. (If there is anything "beyond language"—whatever that expression might mean—it is unsayable and therefore unknowable.) Finally, he is committed to the belief that language includes those regions lying just within and along its frontiers.

I am not suggesting for a moment that an educated Christian today could ever be expected to say what I have just been saying. My analysis of his discourse as edge-language is a description, not a translation or a paraphrase, of a religious man's use of language. The implications of this way of speaking are logical, and it would probably take argument to bring a Christian to see that the cluster of beliefs which we have described is implied by his way of talking.

I am also not suggesting that this cluster of beliefs is implied only by the discourse of Christians, nor that one need be a Christian to hold these convictions about the role and scope of language. They are implications of any of the various ways of speaking at the borders of language. The humorist and the poet are also committed to these beliefs.

Before going further, may we say of this first set of implied beliefs that they—or any one of them—could be false? I think we may. They could be shown to be false by argument, by presenting examples which illustrated and made persuasive some other description of the role and the range of the uses of language. In short, my whole description of language is either right or wrong. It could also be partly right and partly wrong, needing this or that correction, large or small, and suggestions for improving it can only be welcome. It does not seem to be a misuse of words, then, to say that this description of the use of, and our relationship to, language is either true or false.

We may develop further this first set of convictions about the facts of our situation. The Christian is also committed to saying that those who deny, ignore, or avoid the frontiers of language pay the price of living more restricted lives in a more restricted world than does one who sees, affirms, and frequents the frontiers as well as the rest of our language. Their world is more restricted and they live more limited lives because they have excluded much of humor, most of poetry, and all of religion. Whether it is better to live in a clearer but narrower world is another matter, but that that world is narrower is asserted. This assertion, too, is either true or false.

Alasdair MacIntyre, having first defended theism and then sided with the atheists, has more recently decided that the whole debate between theists and atheists is culturally peripheral.[5] I am inclined to agree with his most recent position.[6] Arguments about different ways of being a positivist are hardly newsworthy. I should suggest, however, that the difference between positivists of both sorts and those who are aware of the frontiers of language is a difference of no small cultural moment. As we have said, religious persons are only one small group of those who push out to the edges of language, but this issue is so basic to their religion that they have no choice but to take sides against any sort of positivism. Perhaps their own most culturally useful role, however, on behalf of a fuller life in a wider world, would be to resist positivistic interpretations of their own religion by those who call themselves Christians. That resistance may not make headlines either, but it may in the long run be the necessary prerequisite to putting religion to that service of man which Christians have always thought it should render. It is one of religion's aims to prevent the advance of positivism, not in order to preserve religion, but for the sake of the fullness of human life. It is a matter, the religious man would say (using frontier-language), of the salvation of the world!

The second set of beliefs about our situation implied by Christian edge-language will be no more satisfying than the first to those who have argued that religion has to do with the facts (in the sense of "facts" implied by the verification principle). The second set begins with a belief that is implied by

5. See MacIntyre's essay in *The Religious Significance of Atheism* (New York: Columbia University Press, 1969).
6. But this brings us just as far and no further than the point Hume reached in the last part of his *Dialogues Concerning Natural Religion*, two centuries ago.

the things Christians say, and which they even make explicit from time to time. This is the judgment, or the belief, that the way of life that follows from going to the edges of language in speaking of the history of Israel and of the Israelite Jesus is the *true* way, the way which is right for every man. More than this, they are committed to the conviction that that story shows the truth about human history and about every human being. They believe that this way of speaking of man and the human situation is the truest, the soundest, the most reliable way in which to speak of man—on its own level, of course (no attempt is made to speak of man on the level of the natural sciences, for example). Any other beliefs about man as a social political, and self-understanding being are on the same level as those of religion, however, and there Christians claim that they perceive a truth, not all of the truth, but a truth without which other truths will go astray.

This claim to have discovered the way, the truth, and the life, may be developed to show what it includes. It includes a conception of the world as the scene of human history (whatever else may be said about the world is to be said only after that). History, furthermore, is a struggle of faithfulness, love, justice, and mercy, against self-love, betrayal, injustice, and vengeance. That struggle is portrayed in the story of Israel and of the Israelite Jesus. Going to the very limit of what language allows as sense, the Christian says that this history is the "place" where 'God is made known. And the center of this story, it is further claimed, the climax of this struggle, is the death and resurrection of Jesus.

Question: The death and *what?*
Answer: That God raised Jesus from the dead.
Q: Come now! Do you wish to say that that really happened?
A: Did *what* really happen?
Q: Well are you trying to say that the man was dead and then, that having died, he came back to life again?
A: That was not at all what I said. I can imagine a man dying, and then being resuscitated. It would be strange, and we should want to say that he hadn't really or completely died, because when we think of

someone dying, we think of his story's being over, with no more future—which is more than just the heart stopping. But I want to say that Jesus Christ's history did not stop with his death. I do not really know how to say it, except in some odd phrase like the one I used. So if you are asking me, did his history really continue, then, except for my uncertainty about how much is packed into that "really," I want to say, Yes.

Q: But we do not talk about a man's history unless the man has been around to be seen and felt, talked to and listened to, in short, an agent in human affairs. Are you claiming that that is still the case with Jesus? And if so, what sort of a claim is this? If you take away the empirical evidence of history, it is no longer history.

A: I see your problem. You think I am stretching the word "history" too far. Well, I am not sure I can make sense of this, but let me see what I can say. I could say (and you would understand me then), that his life and teaching continued to influence others, even those who heard about him only later and never knew him before his death. Or I could say that he served as an example to others of what it is to be human. I could say that he became a model for Christians, in the light of which they saw further events, so that whenever evil seemed to triumph over love and justice, but was finally unable to crush it, whenever some good, however small, came out of an evil situation, they saw this as confirming their model. I could say that here is the case which refutes the judgment that only the evil that men do lives after them, for the good that this man did lives still. Yes, I could say all that and you would understand, although you might not necessarily agree. And I could add that this man's life, if we take it as a paradigm, shows that nothing matters more in life than how we stand with respect to our neighbor, whether we serve him or let him take care of himself. Yes, all that I could say.

Now the difficulty arises. It arises for both of us, however. The trouble is that in saying each of these things, I find them inadequate. I want to go further than these words allow. I find myself wanting to say something wild, such as that this man's history lies at the heart of our history here and now and of where we shall all be tomorrow. That doesn't make much sense either, so instead I use those strange old words and say, yes, that God raised Jesus from the dead, a new Israel for every man.

Q: Well, I think I see what you are trying to do, but then we need to consider whether you are making a claim at all. What you are doing, it seems to me, is behaving unreasonably about a bit of ancient history.

A: Yes, I think that is not far from the mark.

Q: But then, it is surely not for reasonable men to behave in such a fashion? With what we know of human history, can we not find other men than Jesus who have contributed much to the human enterprise? And should not a reasonable man then take something from each example, keeping some perspective and balance, finally deciding himself how he is to live? And even were a reasonable man to weight the story of Jesus rather heavily, he would hardly be entitled to speak nonsense in that way.

A: I said you were not far from the mark. But you would have been closer if you had said I was behaving unreasonably about the whole human enterprise. You may say it is unreasonable to care so much about what human beings do to each other, and unreasonable to think that one particular segment of human history provides such special clues. But I do not see that it is unreasonable for a man to want to tell the story of his life, or of his people, or of the human race. If he tries to tell it as a *story*, then he gives dramatic structure to all the evidence. There is nothing unreasonable about doing that; indeed, I think that it is a rather human thing to do. Only, in telling that story I am never satisfied with what I have said or can say, and so I speak of *God* as the beginning, middle, and end of history. If you put all the historical evidence on a computer of immense capacity, I would only say that I was still dissatisfied. I suffer, as you can see, from what the ancients called (and what I am still pleased to call) "divine discontent."

Q: That is your problem. But as for me, I see no grounds for saying that you are making a claim that could be called true or false.

A: You, not I, have used the word "claim," and I let you decide if your own way of using that word applies to my way of talking. But if you say that what I say cannot be true or false, I suggest that you are begging the question, namely, whether truth or falsity are to be used only of what you call claims. The issue, basically, is the reasonableness of "divine discontent." On this we may indeed disagree, but I do not see that either of us can say that the other has no reasons for his position. We can only say that, up to this point at least, each of us believes his own reasons to be the more persuasive.

We may leave the conversation there, I think, on the level of disagreement at which it began and to which it will no doubt return again and again. Nevertheless, the conversation may serve to demonstrate the second "fact" about the world and our human situation to which the Christian is committed. He has a particular (by no means universally held) estimation of the situation, the possibilities, and the problems of the self in society, in the context of the world. He is convinced that this estimation is more adequate than its competitors to the full range of human experience.

Of course, such a conviction does not exclude the value of other ways of speaking of the human situation. Scientific—medical, psychiatric, sociological, and economic—descriptions of particular situations are all useful. If, however, any of these descriptions surrenders its right to describe by adding to its picture the words, "and that is all there is to say," the Christian will insist that there is still more. More to say, but not more of the same, not more on the same level and in the same terms. Rather, he will press for the legitimacy of other ways of speaking, including those which go right to the edges of our language.

Our imagined conversation between a Christian and a questioner has left unsettled whether the Christian was in fact making a claim, and—if he was—of what sort. Could it be said that he is making a metaphysical "claim"? That is, is Christianity a way of seeing the world, of seeing everything, such that it could be classed as a metaphysics? I think not. Religion did have once such grandiose pretensions. It once presumed to offer answers to every question that could be asked, and to be relevant to everything in human life. For the contemporary, educated Christian, however, his religion can no longer accomplish so much, nor does he regret this retrenchment, any more than philosophers seem to regret their own relatively recent more humble estimation of the task of philosophy.

Metaphysics may be conceived as the attempt to describe the structure of our understanding of what is the case, generally, with the world. Or it may be thought of as the attempt to describe the workings of language when we say, "This is how things are." Or again, metaphysics may be thought of as one or another proposal for seeing in a particular way everything which we have been looking at already. On any of these lines, the first set of beliefs implicit in Christian discourse (and also in any other use of language at its frontiers) may be judged to be a metaphysical judgment. However, this metaphysical judgment is not peculiarly that of the Christian, as we have seen. When we come to judgments which are peculiarly those of Christians, as we do with our second set of beliefs, then we come to a way of saying how *some* things are, or better, how some aspects of some things are, a proposal for seeing some things in a certain way. The contemporary, educated Christian does not claim that he has anything special to say in many situations or on any number of matters, from meteorology to mining engineering. For the areas in which he thinks he does have something important to say, he will, if he is reflective, have to work out his metaphysical underpinnings like any other man. I have indicated with what I called the first set of implied beliefs (and more fully in Chapters III and IV) the underpinnings which seem adequate to develop a proper understanding of what the Christian is up to, in speaking as he does.

It seems, then, that the religion of the educated Christian today leads him to hold specific and concrete views on those subjects that touch what we have called the history of man: his social, political, economic life in the world, with its known, if disputed, past and its unknown future. When a subject touches any aspect of the human story and how it is to be told (a large and important part of our life and language, making up at least three-fourths of human life) the Christian may or may not speak, but he will surely have something to say and his own way of saying it. Nonetheless, the interests of religion and of metaphysics are not the same, even if there is some overlapping. Although it is intimately related to both, religion is no more metaphysics than it is morality.

EPILOGUE
The Logic of a Religion

Throughout this study our concern has been to make clear the logic of one particular religion by providing an accurate description of what is going on when a contemporary, educated Christian speaks in a manner characteristic of his religion—up to and including his way of using the word 'God.' We have tried to show that what he is doing is not accurately described by saying that he is making statements about facts, although it is not to be denied that he is concerned about the facts. Nor is his activity well described as expressing or commending an intention to behave in a certain way, although it is not to be denied that such an intention is intimately related to his speech. Nor is the Christian making metaphysical assertions when he says, in his own way, that God is love or that Christ is Lord of history, although he does hold certain beliefs about what is the case with our human situation, which may be inferred from his manner of speaking, once it is rightly understood. No, he is engaging in a special type of linguistic behavior which we have described as speaking at the edges of language. The logic of this particular linguistic behavior is what we have aimed to make clear.

In the course of clarifying the logic of this religion, we have also tried to show the nature and the source of some of the most common misunderstandings of religion. The mistaken view with which we dealt primarily is the one that leads to the conflict between theism and atheism. Both of these positions,

167

we have tried to show, depend upon a too narrow conception of the ways in which our language works. An inadequate view of the workings of language has led, understandably, to inadequate descriptions of religious discourse.

If our description is along the correct lines, if what we have presented in our analysis is in any way the logic of this religion, it becomes possible to see what is the issue posed by religion, what sort of a "choice" religion presents, and therefore how it is that reasonable men and women today can and do make that choice. The issue is not whether to be rational or irrational. Reasons of various sorts and weights can be offered on either side, as we saw, so that the difference between those who reject and those who accept religion is not between more and less reasonable men. Nor is the issue posed by the difference between holding to older or more modern "world-views." The decision is not whether to reject or accept the features of transience, plurality, relativity, and autonomous human responsibility that mark contemporary Western culture. If one has those features in mind in calling ours a secular culture, then the Christian may be as little or as much secular as any of the rest of us.

The issue, rather, is about how to speak, whether to use words in certain ways, and therefore at the same time about how to live, how linguistically to inhabit our world. The choice about religion is the choice between residing exclusively in language's central plains, and exploring out to some of its frontiers. To be a Christian is to go to certain edges of language and to push there at its limits. More specifically, to be a Christian is to go to those limits in telling the story of all men, in the light of, as a further stage in, and under the judgment and promise of, the story which Israel told of its own history and which some first-century Jews told about the Jew Jesus. Such behavior is not required by our culture nor by whatever philosophy we may hold about the nature of man. There is nothing naturally, historically, or logically necessary about making this decision. It is, however, a decision which can be (and not infrequently is) made by intelligent human beings.

If I am anywhere near the right track in so analyzing the discourse of Christians, then it can be seen that accepting the religion under consideration is not only feasible but also desirable. There are those who make this choice and thereby find what they call a more abundant life. I do not mean that all who call themselves Christians choose Christianity in the form which we have been examining. As we said at the beginning, many forms are covered by the loose term "Christianity." Nevertheless, the choice which we are considering is one which can appeal to a reasonable man today, especially if the principal alternatives presented to him are those of theism and atheism. Neither of those alternatives is sufficiently independent of the positivistic tendencies at work in our culture to be able to challenge them in a significant way. If the narrow perspectives of positivism are judged to be inadequate to the full scope of human potentiality, no broadening of vision can be expected from two such common children of that same narrowness.

We have seen humor, poetry, and human love to be behavior logically similar to that of religion, and each can only regard the others as allies in the cultural battle to make room for man. While each is valuable in its own right and on its own terms, the Christian will tend to judge that none of these deals as centrally as does his religion with the great questions of our time: whether the human experiment is to continue and whether, if it does, it will be more or less human.

The central issue of our culture and society, as the Christian could be expected to see it, is the issue of human history: how it is to be told, how it is to be lived, and whether it has a future. His religion leads him to focus his concern on (or we could say, it consists in his concern to go to the limit of language in speaking of) the human story, as it also leads him to engage himself (or, again, consists in his engaging himself) in the living and making of that story. In behaving thus, he may help to keep open the full range of human possibilities of life and language. If that is a desirable end, then his choice is not only feasible but one which can be commended. Other

versions of Christianity may have their contributions to make
as well, but if they are properly described by a theistic interpretation, then their contribution, whatever it may be claimed
to be, will hardly be as relevant to our culture as that of the
form of Christianity which we are considering. A religion that
is not at its heart an acknowledgment of, and a participation in,
using the edges of language can hardly be expected to stand
against the positivistic pressures of the culture in which we
live.

Finally, the description that we have made of characteristic
speech-acts of Christians raises a question about our way of
understanding religion, and about most contemporary philosophy of religion, and thus it is a question for contemporary
philosophy. There has been much talk about talk in recent
philosophy, and so, much talk about "religious language" in
the philosophy of religion. But our analysis makes clear that
there is no such entity as "religious language." There is only
our human language, whether English, French, or some other,
and then there is all the rich variety of the things we do in,
with, and through our language. One of the many uses of language is that which the religious man makes in using the word
'God' as he does. This use, however (if our analysis of it is
anywhere near right), does raise the question whether we have
in fact made our way around "the linguistic turn," whether
the so-called revolution in philosophy has not, like so many
revolutions of the past, only produced a situation in which the
same old tyrannies are exercised under new coverings, rather
than producing the promised freedom for better understanding. It may be that Wittgenstein and Austin led us to the
mountain from which a new land of understanding became
visible, or from which some very ancient terrain could be
seen in a quite new way. In spite of all the talk of "ordinary
language" and language as "rule-governed behavior," however, little enough has been made of this new perspective,
little progress has been made into the promised land so
revealed. That is why we devoted so much space in this
investigation to language as our distinctively human way of

being in the world. Yet it is just this perspective, as I believe this analysis shows, which can give us a clearer view of our subject.

The task of winning that clearer view, however, has only been begun in these pages. Much of what I have done here now needs the far more careful attention and the more finely drawn distinctions that Austin, especially, tried to teach us to exercise and draw. We have painted the scene with a big brush and used too rapid and long strokes. We have done so in order to open the way for a more accurate description of the workings of language as used characteristically by an educated, Western Christian today. Insofar as this rough description has begun along the right lines, to that extent we hope to have made a contribution to the clearer understanding of the logic of one religion and perhaps to the logic of others.

Indexes

Name Index

Subject Index